AF478164

Rainer Fetting
Los Angeles Surfscapes

RAINER

FETTING

LOS

ANGELES

SURFSCAPES

KERBER VERLAG

Rainer Fetting   **Karl Pfefferle**

You spent three months in Los Angeles and painted 25 mostly small sized pictures.
We are showing nearly the complete series in our exhibition »Los Angeles Surfscapes«. I am interested in your relationship to the sea. Is there something special about the sea which fascinates you? In addition to many other subjects you have repeatedly featured in your paintings, the sea crops up constantly.

I already painted pictures of the sea when I lived in Wilhelmshaven. That is a long time ago now. The first paintings, with the breakers thrashing against the pier, that was in 1973.

You were 24, in other words just starting out.

But I painted pictures of the sea before that. For instance, when the Jadebusen (an inlet near Bremerhaven) was iced up in winter I painted the boats in the harbor and the ice floes.

Is it nature that fascinates you or more the force of nature that moves you? After all, you can associate more with the sea than just the feeling of distance, longing, expanse.

Well, I tend to think visually. When I paint pictures I don't formulate them verbally in advance. I suppose I extract them from my visual database. If I were to put into words today why I painted

these paintings back then, I can remember for example that when I painted the car on Wilhelmshaven Pier in 1973, I was influenced by the English artist William Turner. I had discovered his
paintings in the National Gallery in London and was hugely fascinated by his sea paintings and
shipwrecks. It was this dramatic aspect that interested me, and how the paintings were painted.

That was going to be the second part of my question. Are you saying it was not only nature itself
that stirred your interest in the sea but also other artists' works?

Yes, I am positive. And Turner was your earliest influence? Or did more modern artists such as Emil Nolde also
influence you in some way?

I first got to know Nolde during my childhood. I was confronted
with art, especially with the Expressionists such as Emil Nolde on
account of my father, who had shelves full of books and reproduc-
tions. Nolde later lived in Schleswig Holstein, where the country is
just as flat as in Wilhelmshaven and East Friesia, in other words
monotonous. And so I instilled it with drama in »Sturmsituationen«
(»Storm Situations«) or »Auto and Liebespaar bei stürmischer See«
(»Car and Lovers During Stormy Sea«).

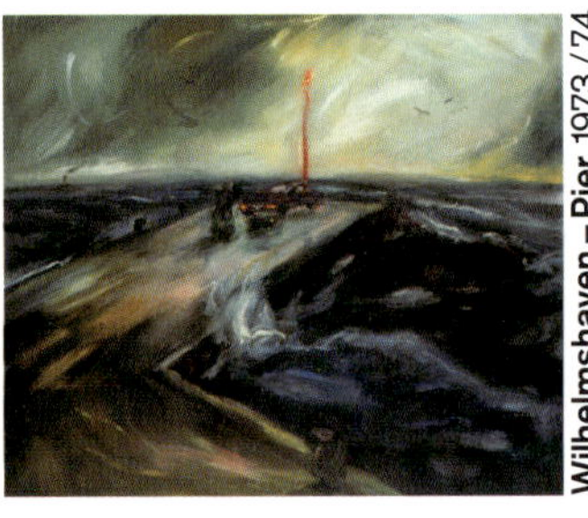

Wilhelmshaven – Pier 1973 / 74

But the drama is not that intense in Nolde, is it?

Well, yes it is, due to the color contrasts as well. I find Nolde's landscapes intensely dramatic
and heightened by the stark contrasts. As you know I have since done away with Expressionist
elements in my paintings. So you won't see that many lilac skies in them; I think this influence
might have come from "photorealism'.

Yet there is still exaggeration?

Yes, owing to my having painted the rough, choppy sea. The breakers thrashing against the pier,
the rough sea, and the cutters struggling through the waves, or the ice, when the harbor is iced
up. That is what is so interesting, the ice floes breaking up and piling on top of each other.
I already featured this topic in the paintings I did as a child.

Which makes me think of a painting you yourself mentioned already – with the car standing on the
jetty. It is actually a painting of which previously there have been no examples in art history.

Which is why I painted it. Because such a modern car, whose tail-light is reflected in the water on the jetty, would never have been painted by Nolde.

The way the car is standing there is actually quite dangerous. Or is that not necessarily the case?

Well, no. It gives you the feeling that something might happen. It is not a painting you would walk past indifferently…

Anyway, to move on to the surfer paintings in the exhibition. How did they come about?

The older I get the more I need water, because I come from by the sea. Water has always helped me recharge my batteries and achieve a balance to my stressful life in the city and my profession. When you paint in oils you are constantly dealing with toxins, something that outsiders, who only ever see the result, an attractive painting, do not realize. Especially when you are working on large-sized paintings the fumes from turpentine and the toxins in paint cause headaches, skin problems and other physical discomfort. That is why I try to mitigate the effects as much as possible by cycling in the fresh air. The sea is especially healing because it cleans the bronchial tubes and respiratory tract. That is why when living in smog-ridden Los Angeles I felt the need to at least move close to the sea, down in Venice Beach, which has a village-like feel to it. You also have the city, the movie metropolis as well as a decent gallery scene close by.

And the surfing topic is just par for the course, given the number of surfers out there on the water.

That's another reason. So you just go down to the beach and start drawing? I noticed you have sketchpads full of drawings of surfers, some of them really tiny, notes as it were.

I needed a break from Berlin and I felt drawn to the sea, but the sea in a city. First of all I just relaxed there, and it was then I discovered the surfers and started making sketches of them in a small pad. Did you actually have any contact to the surfers there?

No, I didn't. And you never tried surfing yourself?

I never wanted to expose myself to the danger of adventure sports. My adrenaline levels are quite high in my job each day. I don't need an extra kick.

In fact, paintings depicting sports are a rarity in art. You don't see pictures of mountaineers or parachutists as you do maybe in adverts or on movie placards. Were you intrigued by the thought of plunging headlong into a topic that is not well regarded in art?

Not well received? That really does not bother me. Nor is that the reason I painted them. I have no idea why something like that should not be painted. Are the paintings perhaps not profound or intellectual enough because they only focus on sport? I can't relate to that.

Do the uplifted arms in the painting »L.A. surfscape IV« signalize danger?

No, the surfers want to get past the wave. Some people dive through it because they don't want to be caught up in its sheer force, or if possible, if it is not too strong, they force themselves over it. And when you raise your arms they absorb the wave's resistance. It is about man's struggle with the universe. In contrast, pelicans hover effortlessly, exploiting the lift above the waves. People become small in the surf. Small figures waging battle with nature. All of a sudden that intrigued me. Previously, I would paint surf pictures that only showed the sea, where you only see the sea's force. Then for the first time I started to add people, who actually move about in these waves.

Basically that is an age-old topic facing humanity; man alone out at sea, alone even in boats. Naturally, in 17th-century Dutch painting it is the entire crew, but it is nonetheless alone at sea.

Yes, that's another similarity with Turner. Where the battleships go up in flames and sink, and in my case it is just individual persons.

So it's the topic of existence.

Yes, people are more individuals these days. You don't need to show entire battleships going up in flames.

An American documentary film on the history of surfing has just hit French movie theaters. Stacy Peralta has spliced old shots and shows this very unique surfing culture. When World War II was over young men came back from Europe, had no job to go to and so lots of them hung around in the cities. Others said let's go West and live where the waves are, go fishing and lead a romantic lifestyle of sorts – but with the constant danger surfing involves. An intriguing lifestyle.

There is also another film. But it is already 15 years old now. »Point Break« by Kathryn Bigelow. She was part of the young artist and filmmaker scene back when I was also in New York in 1978. Which is how our paths crossed briefly. I was making my Super 8 movie »Brooklyn 11238«. Kathryn Bigelow later discovered the Wooster Group actor Willem Dafoe for it. She made that the movie with Patrick Swayze and Keanu Reeves and it also takes place in this freaky, you could even say criminal, dropout milieu.

Surfing might even be a metaphor for an artist's existence. In actual fact, your becoming interested in this topic seems fairly logical to me. Dangerous in the figurative sense. Descent is possible, the artist's descent into triviality?

If you can talk of triviality in this context I suppose the difference is that artists analyze and represent these things.

Surfing is a subject that involves both drama and violence, and the large format is your forte. What is amazing is that you have also produced extremely small paintings. I would imagine it is just as much of a challenge to work in small sizes as in large ones. You have to omit gesture, which is the very aspect that lends your large-sized paintings – that you still produce simultaneously – a certain individual dynamism. Yet though these surfer paintings are very small, they nonetheless still have this dynamism. As I see it, your ability to be so to the point in a concise format is a direct result of the experience you gained over the last thirty years.

Yes, I would definitely agree that my long years of experience are a contributing factor, though I also produced small-sized paintings previously. It was my exploration of American abstract Expressionism that inspired me to work in large formats.

One thing that struck me is the great variety of paintings in the surfer series. Apart from the dramatic ones there are also pictures with a high level of abstraction. Bearing in mind how the artist plunges headlong into this topic you might think everything would have to be crowded together in one kind of painting.

Maybe I am too nervous and at the same time too organized to express that in one single painting. In the same way that the sea is sometimes angry and sometimes calm, I have to paint a special situation in different paintings. With these really small paintings, which are very condensed, you run the risk of including too much, and swamping things. Indeed, I took great pains to subdue and contain things, make them more monochrome. By zooming into the picture as you would with a photo, you can reduce what is included. You omit background details and just show the essentials. However, zooming in on a subject automatically highlights new details.

There are two other works that are also very unusual. I am thinking of the paintings of the quiet lifeguard stand.

It was the monochrome aspect that interested me in those two paintings with the calm lifeguard stand; in fact, it is also monochrome in reality. On certain days there is this monochrome silvery blue light.   Although you can also see it as an abstract painting, as an experiment with shapes and proportions, I mean surfaces such as you get in...

Mark Rothko. Yes. Mark Rothko.

      Exactly. The reason I find this aspect so important is that the manner in which your work is generally received is very narrow. People often view it solely in a wild, emotional context.

Yes, I have seen a lot of good painting in museums and exhibitions, and I am always primarily inspired by the sensuality a picture exudes and the artist's concentration during its execution. There is for me a linear, further development through the history of art, let's say starting from Diego Velázquez, who has always been one of my favorite artists, via Francisco Goya, Eduard Manet, Paul Cézanne, Vincent van Gogh, Pablo Picasso, Mark Rothko through to Andy Warhol. In each epoch a sensual approach was used to present the prevailing climate of the time in a nutshell.   With the aim of stimulating the observer.

I have been stimulated by paintings, and this is precisely the effect I wish to achieve with my own. Achieving with painting what authors achieve with the written word or musicians with compositions and music.

      Are you saying that creating the painting produces a state of excitement in you?

No, not the actual production.

      You are quite cool?

Well, unfortunately it is not a case of instinctive, gestural painting or the like as the cliché would have us believe. These things have to be evolved using artistic means. You can't get away with doodling or smearing paint around.

      Yet relying solely on technical ability would not suffice either.

That would be a copy.

      Precisely.

You have to elaborate the essential using artistic devices. To my mind the great artists such as Picasso, van Gogh or the others I mentioned always focused on the essential in their paintings.

They used paintings own dynamics to present the essence of a thing.

In an interview with Sibylle Kretschmer you mentioned Dalí, who excels as regards technique, has a strongly narrative element but…

His style is perhaps a little boring. What you have is the execution of the content, but the painting has no life in itself. Colour is blended into colour. It looks technically pretty maybe, but it is boring.

His fantastic creations. You could say this erudition has precedence over the form of the painting.

True, but people had never seen anything like that before. Take clocks that look more like cloths and are suspended from branches or those enormous elephants strutting around like giraffes. That is amusing the first time around, but then the painting loses its tension, its inner life.

Apart from the paintings in the surfer series, which are more abstract, there are also some that employ an almost classic painting style.

Classic. What do you mean by classic?

What I mean is…

You are probably thinking of what you have already seen in other paintings, Turner included.

Yes, but also this complete turnaround in painting. Theme and painting become so fused they can barely be separated from each other. This eddy of colors is actually transformed in the mind to eddies of water. And indeed many artists have solved this in their own way. You go about it differently in your own individual way.

Yes, I allow things to develop from the act of painting and also from coincidence. You have to recognize coincidences like this that arise during painting, and integrate them. Good painting comes from concentrating it, by releasing it.

Painting is your medium but you do not use it as a stylistic device. In other words, not with ironic twists and mind games. That makes your work part of centuries-old painting tradition. Or would you classify yourself more…

Sounds rather upright. I suppose that is what you would call classic, which is not to be confused with academic, which is merely a copy. In other words, classic is based on the starkly sensual painting of great painters which is then infused with its own dynamism and transferred to our time.

Yes, exactly. In the L.A. series there is a Mulholland Drive painting. Does it maybe have something to do with David Lynch's film? Or how did the painting come about?

There is something magic about the name and place. I actually drove there thinking I might maybe run into Marlon Brando, who lives there. Jack Nicholson lives next door. Both men, like James Dean and Robert de Niro, are brilliant actors from the famous Actors Studio in New York I myself thought about applying to in 1978. This method acting was revolutionary at the time and turned traditional Hollywood acting upside down. Actors had to use their own powers of imagination and skills at analysing emotions to imagine themselves in other roles and thus create such a character. In other words, you had to do some soul-searching. Maybe I realized deep down that because I have followed the cinematic scene very closely through to Martin Scorsese (»Taxi Driver«, »Mean Streets«) and contemporary directors like Michael Mann (»Heat«, »Collateral«), I absorbed some essential stuff, and it was also absorbed in my painting. That is why, after Brando's death, you could say I paid tribute to him. He appeared in many films with Rod Steiger (e.g.,»The Pawnbroker«, »In the heat of the night«). I painted Brando from a scene in »On the waterfront«. You can take a look at the result in the Brando-Steiger paintings series.

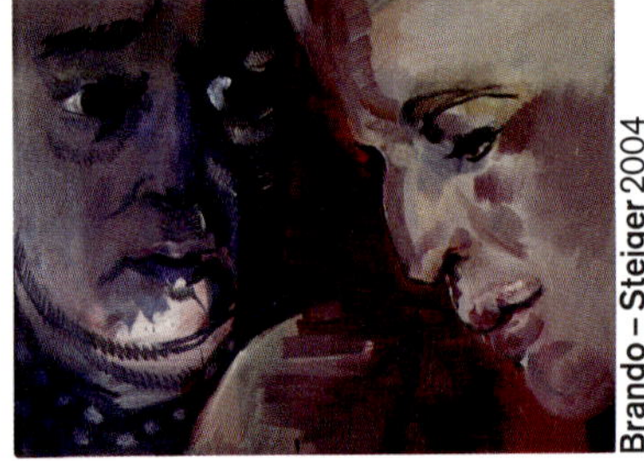

Illustrations I

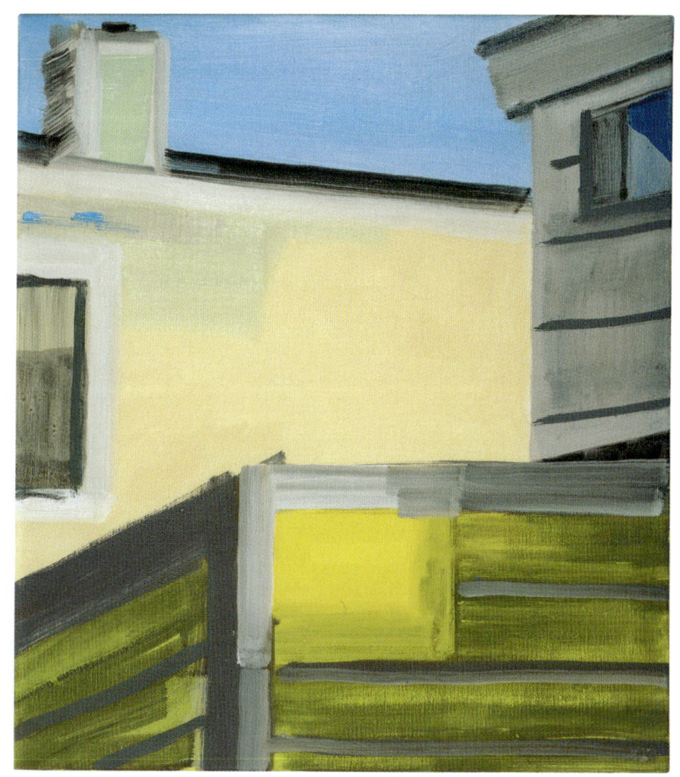

L.A. Sunspot Architecture, 2004

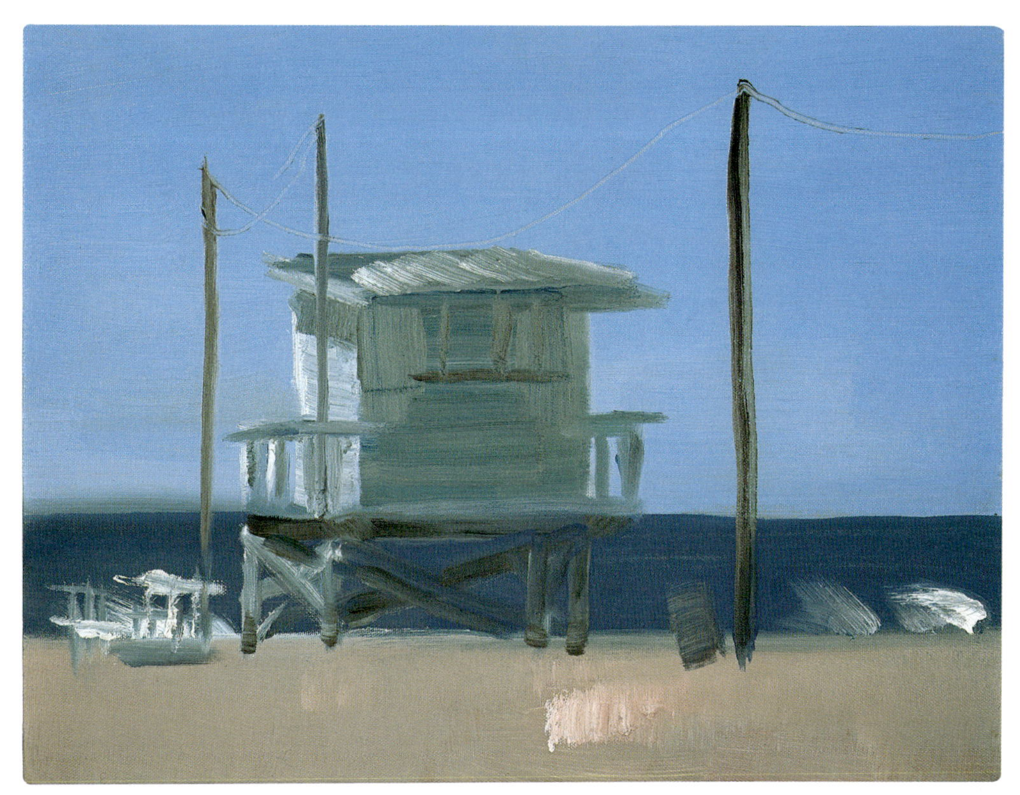

L.A. Lifeguard Stand, 2004

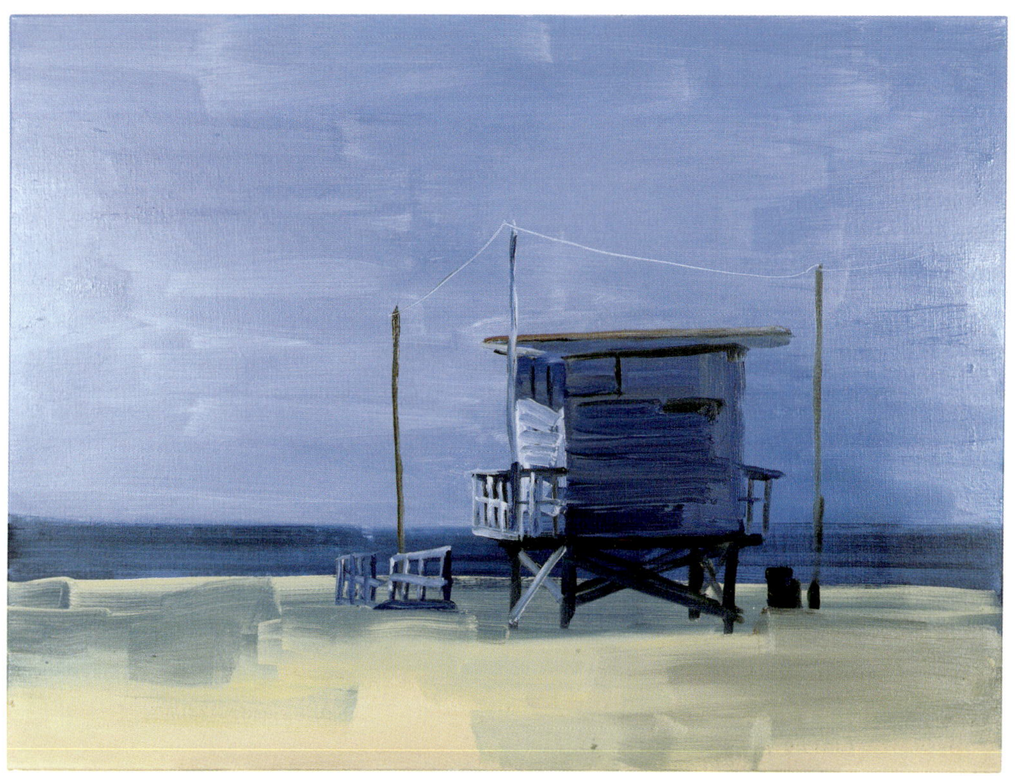

 L.A. Lifeguard Stand, 2004

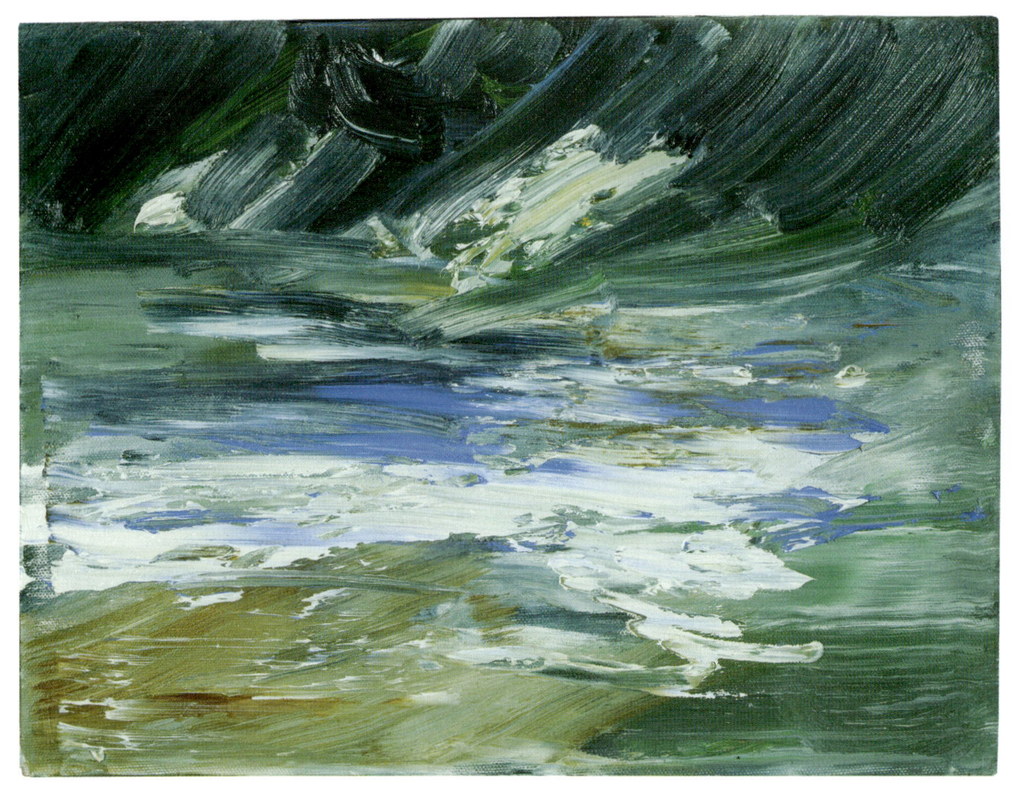

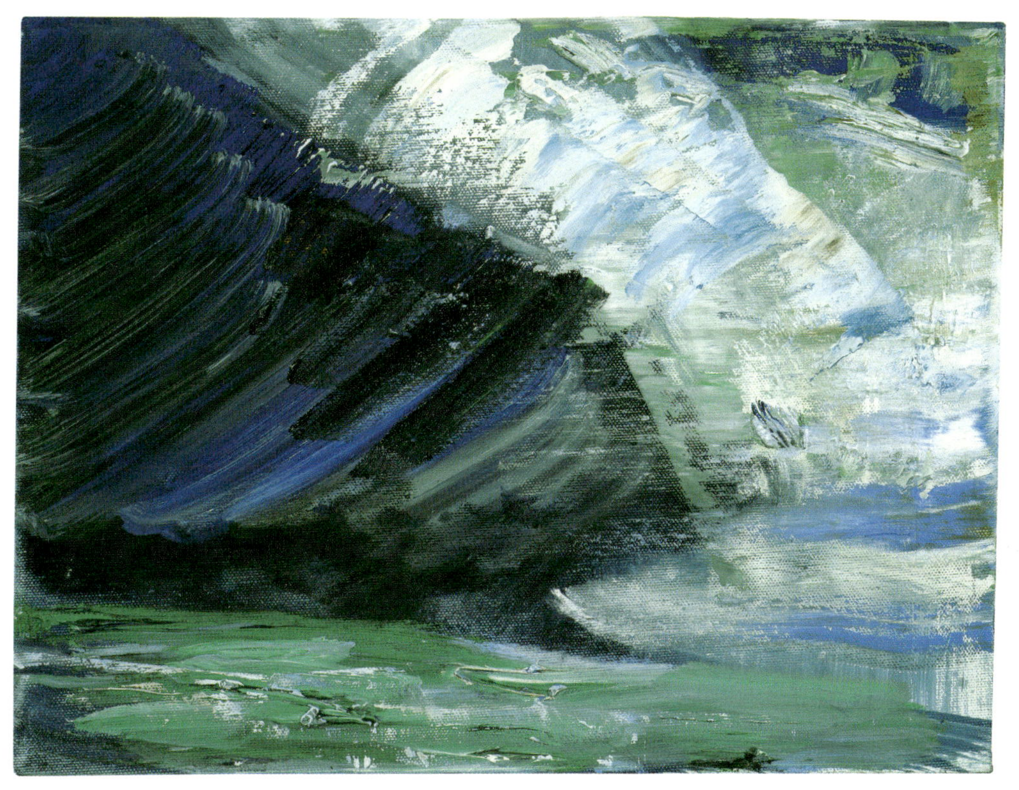

21   L.A. Seascape, 2004

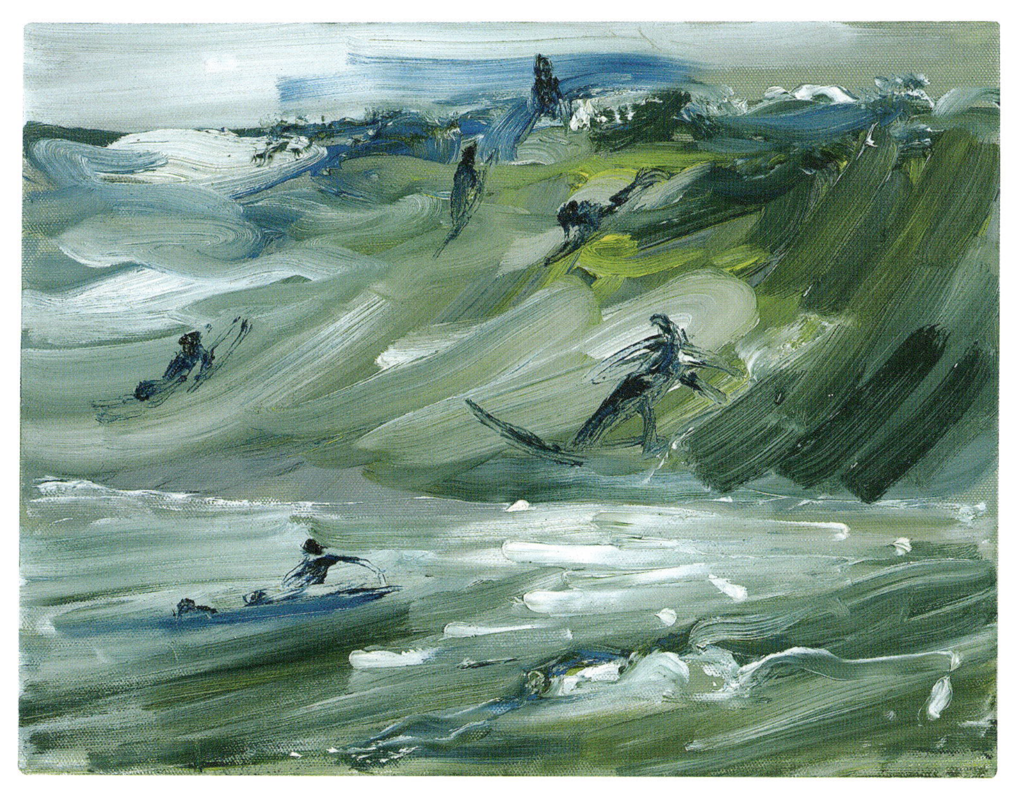

L.A. Surfscape VI, 2004

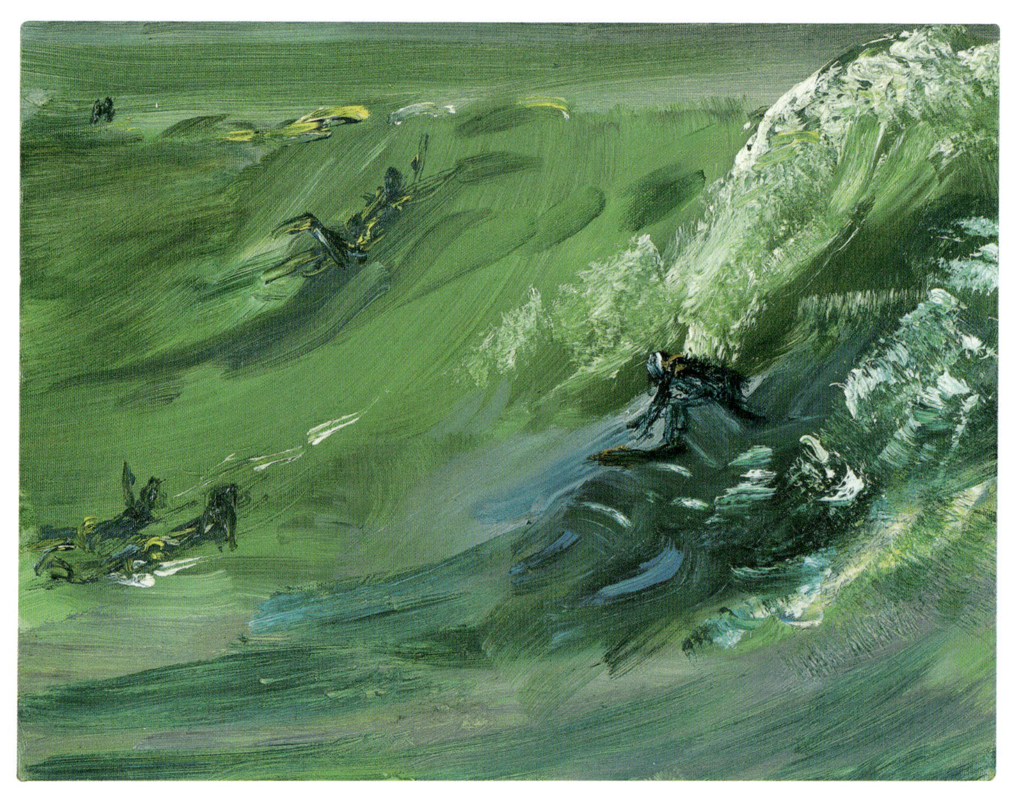

L.A. Surfscape VII, 2004

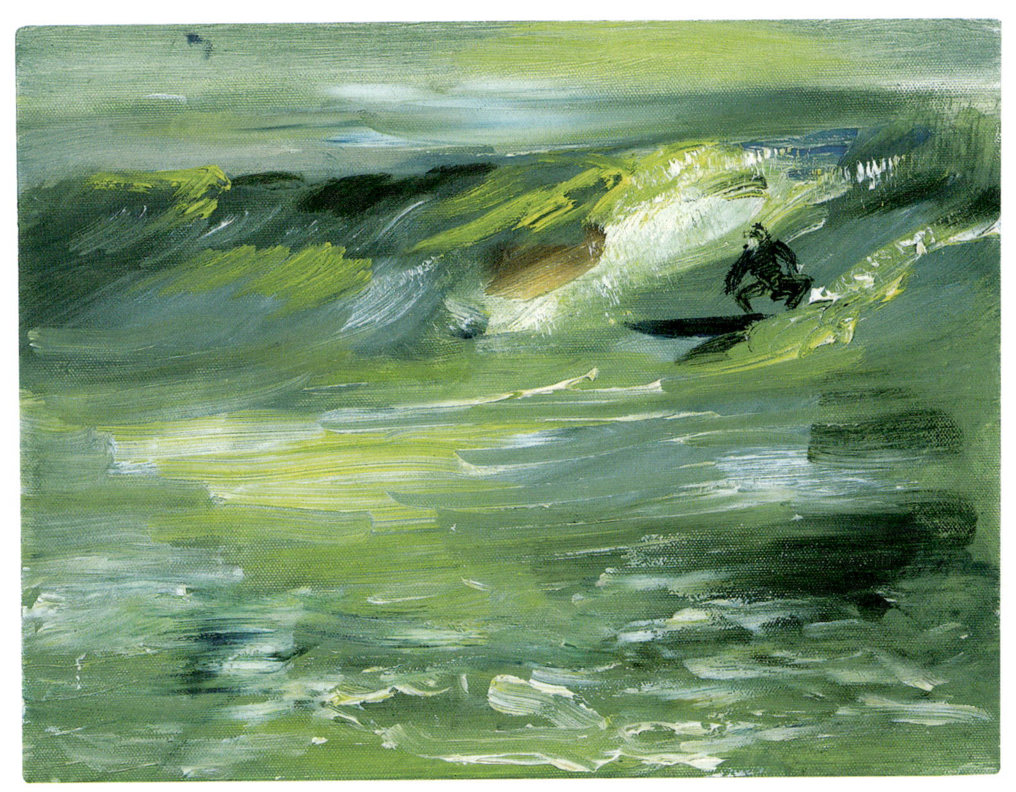

  L.A. Surfscape III, 2004

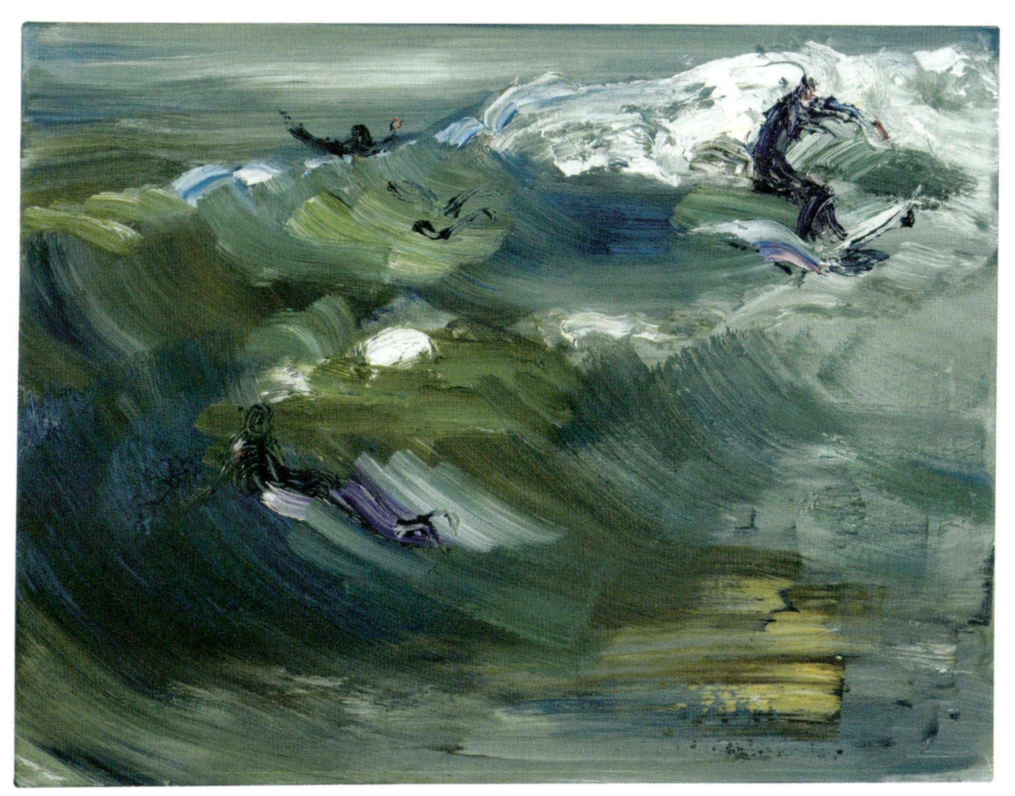

27   L. A. Surfscape IX, 2004

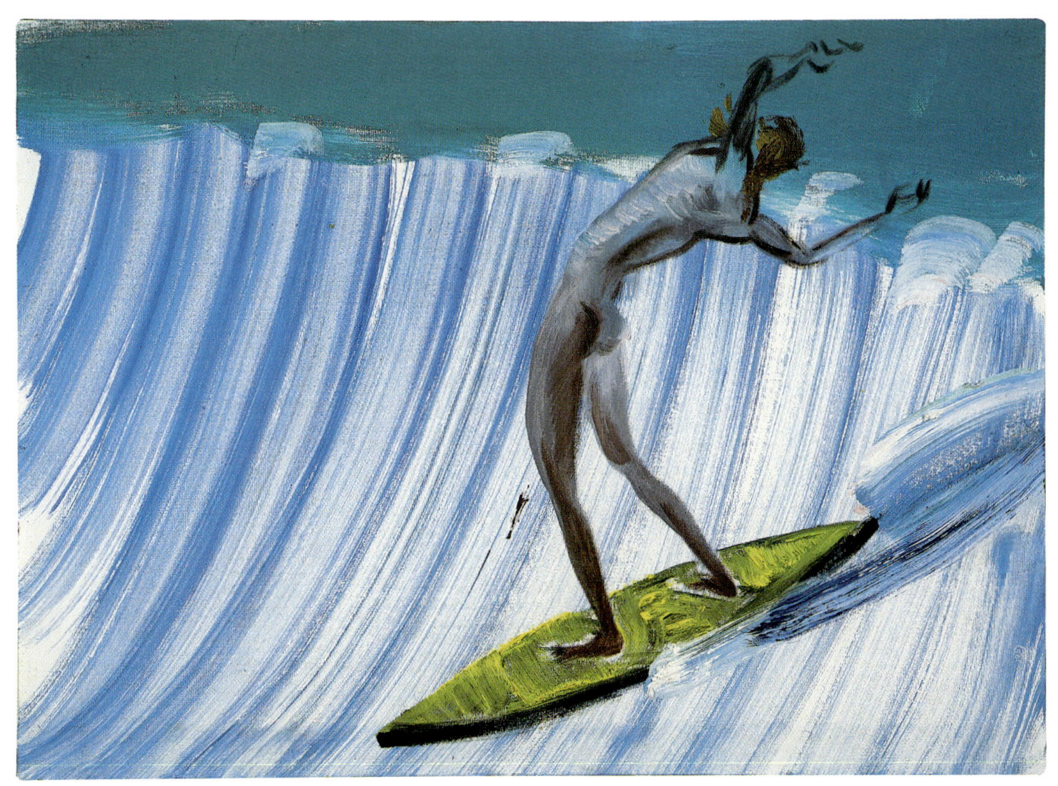

L.A. Surfer Boy, 2004

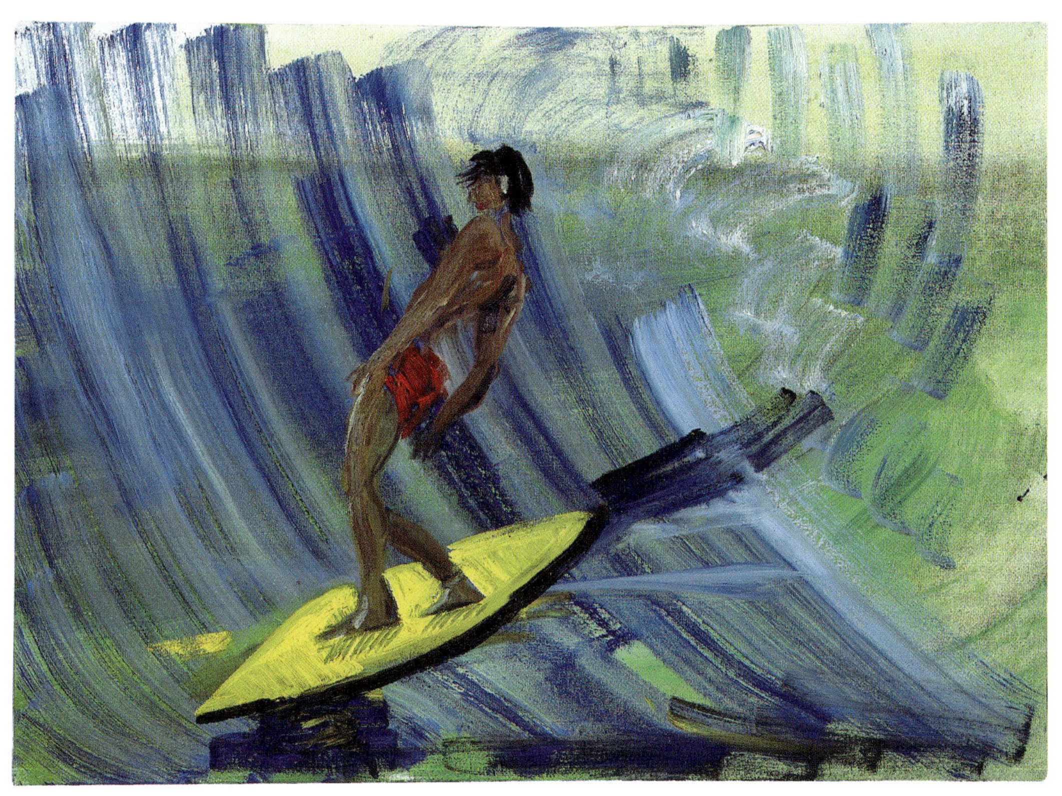

     L.A. Surfer Boy, 2004

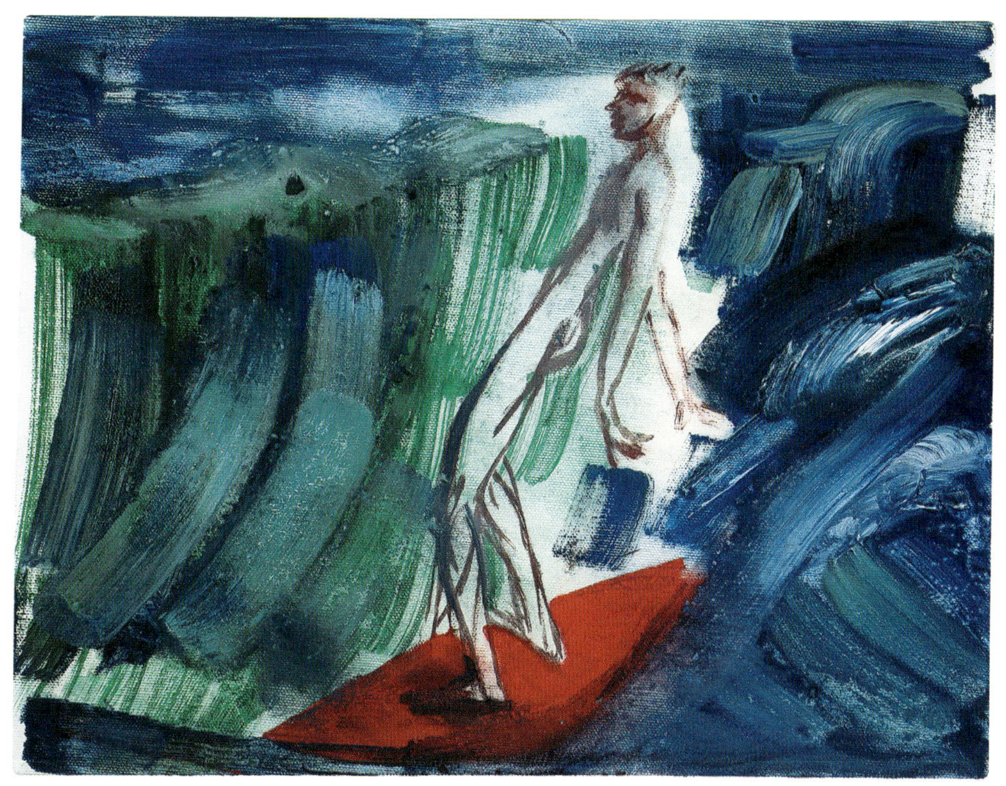

33   L.A. Surfer Boy, 2004

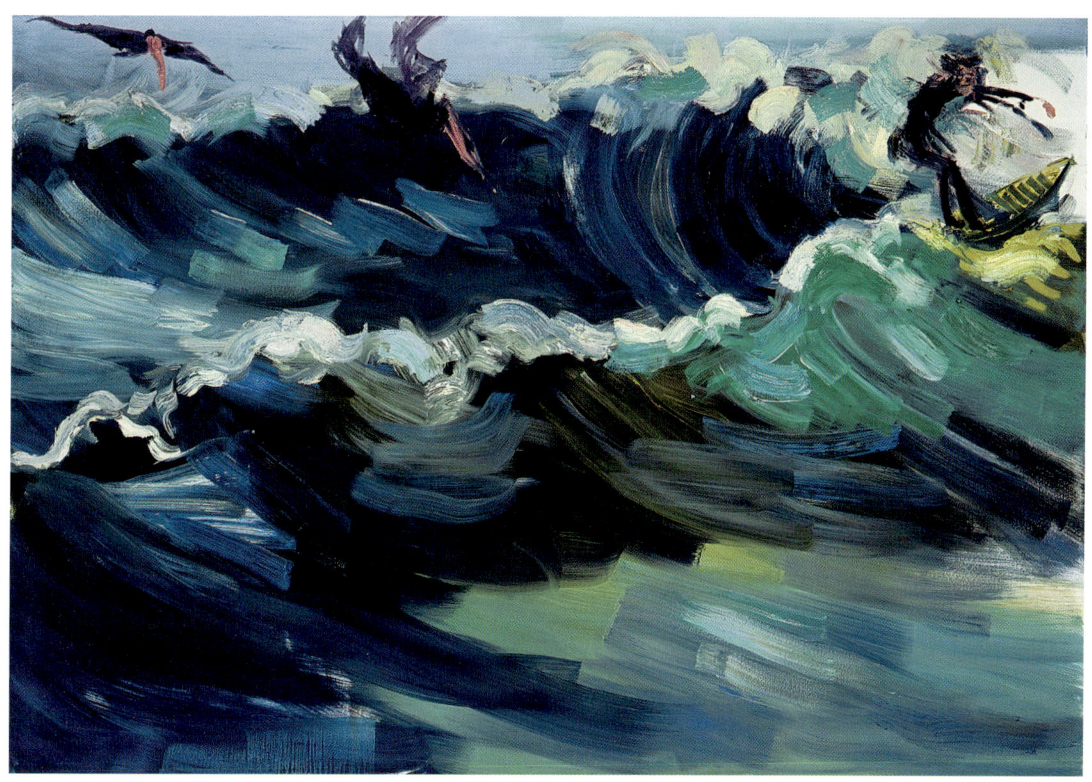

35 L.A. Large Surfscape with Pelicans, 2004

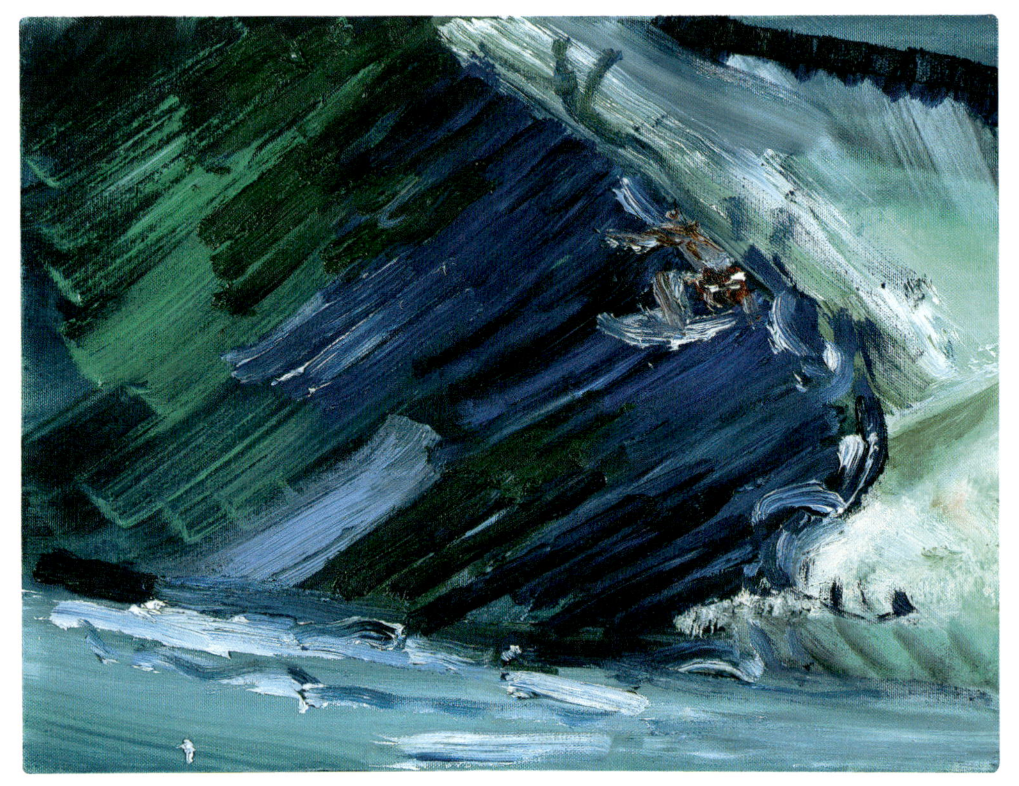

L.A. Surfscape XI, 2004

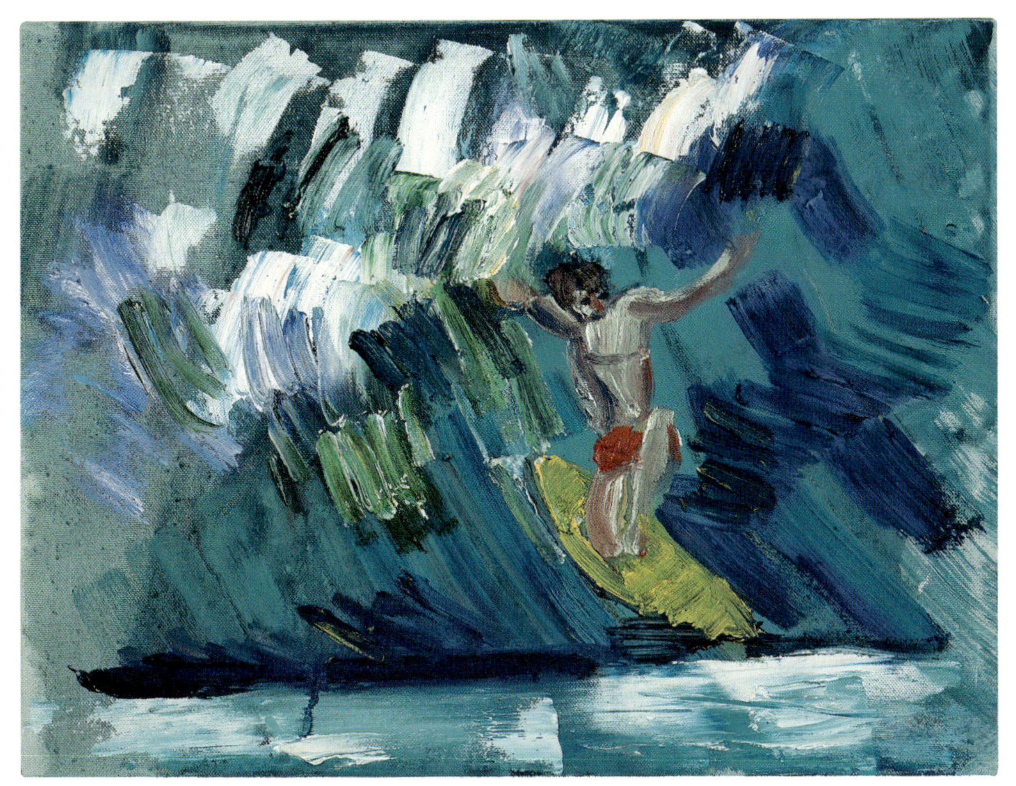

   L.A. Surfscape X, 2004

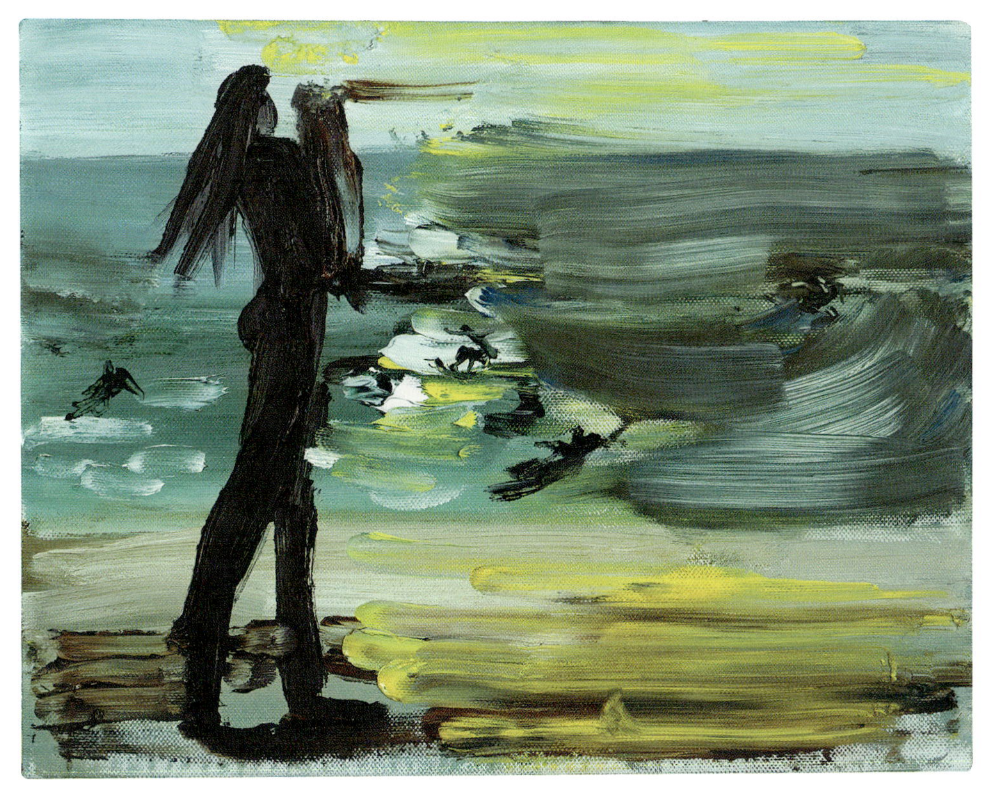

L.A. Surfscape I, 2004

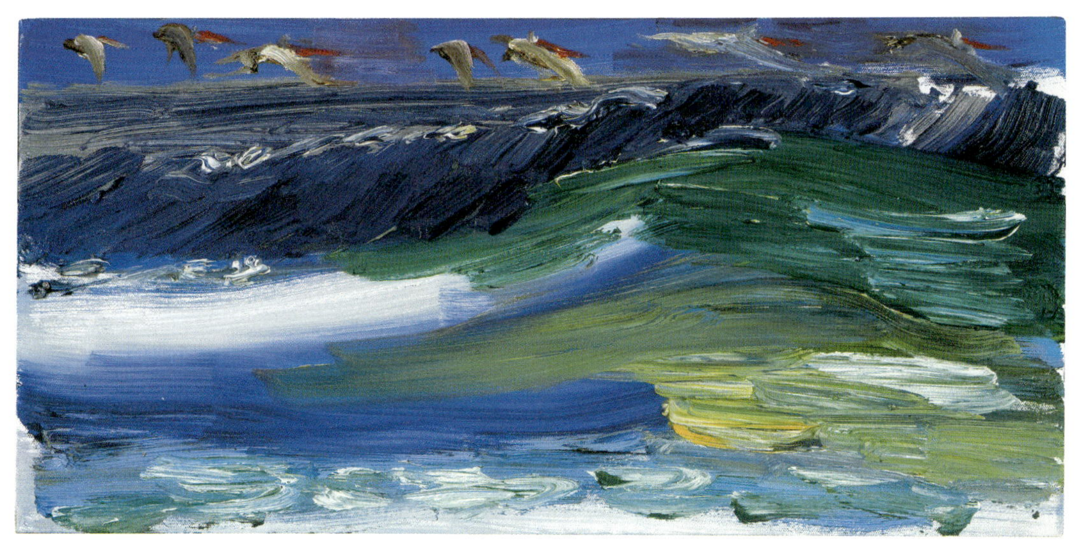

41   L.A. Seascape with Pelicans, 2004

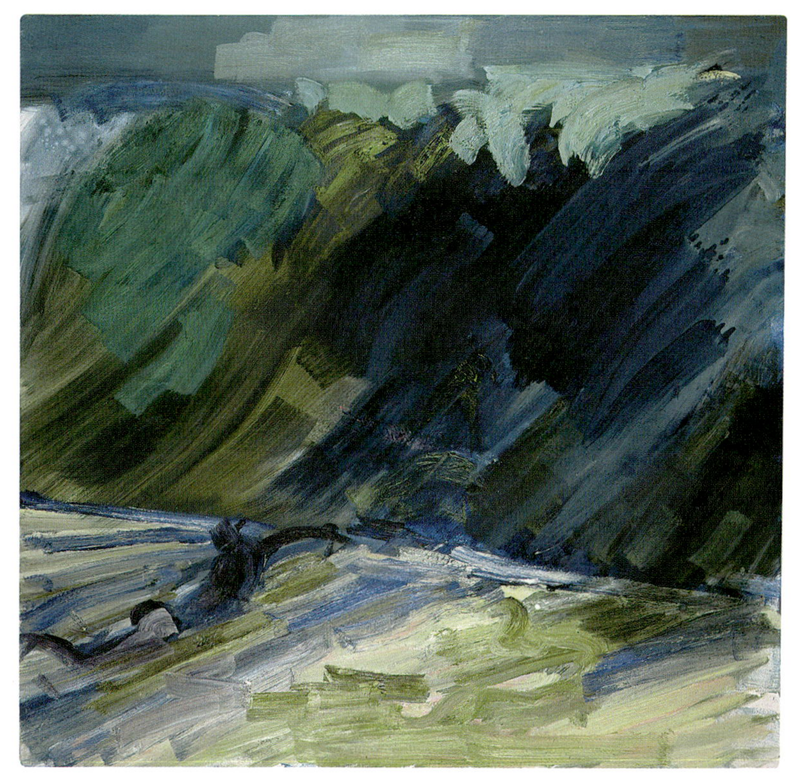

    L.A. Large Surfscape, 2004

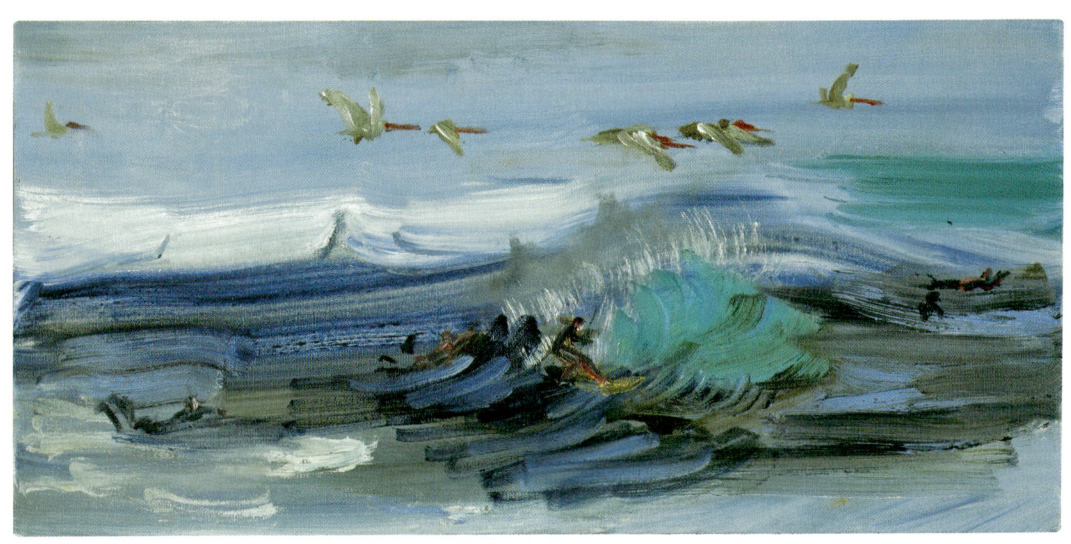

L.A. Seascape with Pelicans, 2004

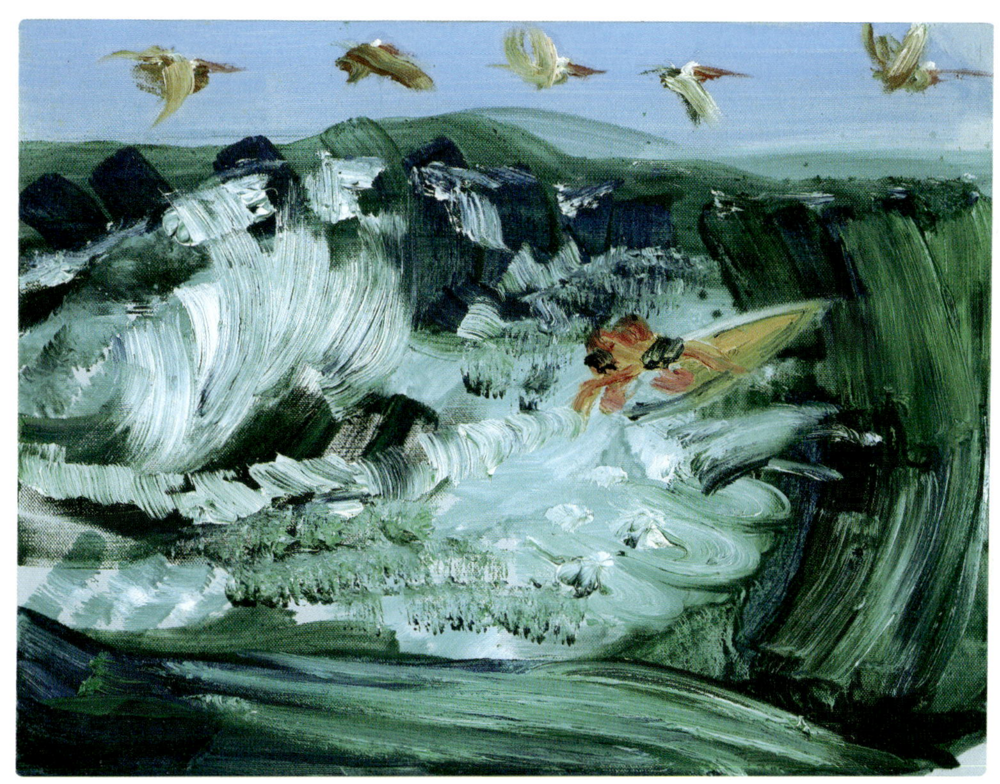

 L.A. Surfscape with Pelicans, 2004

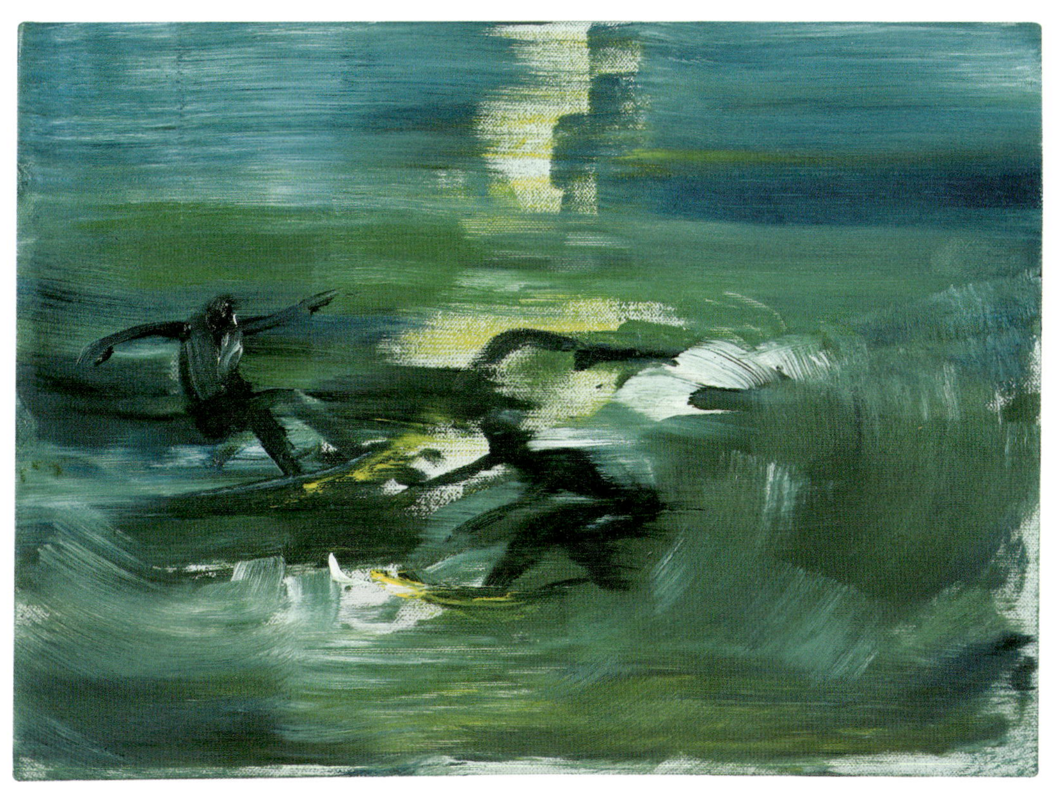

47   L.A. Surfscape II, 2004

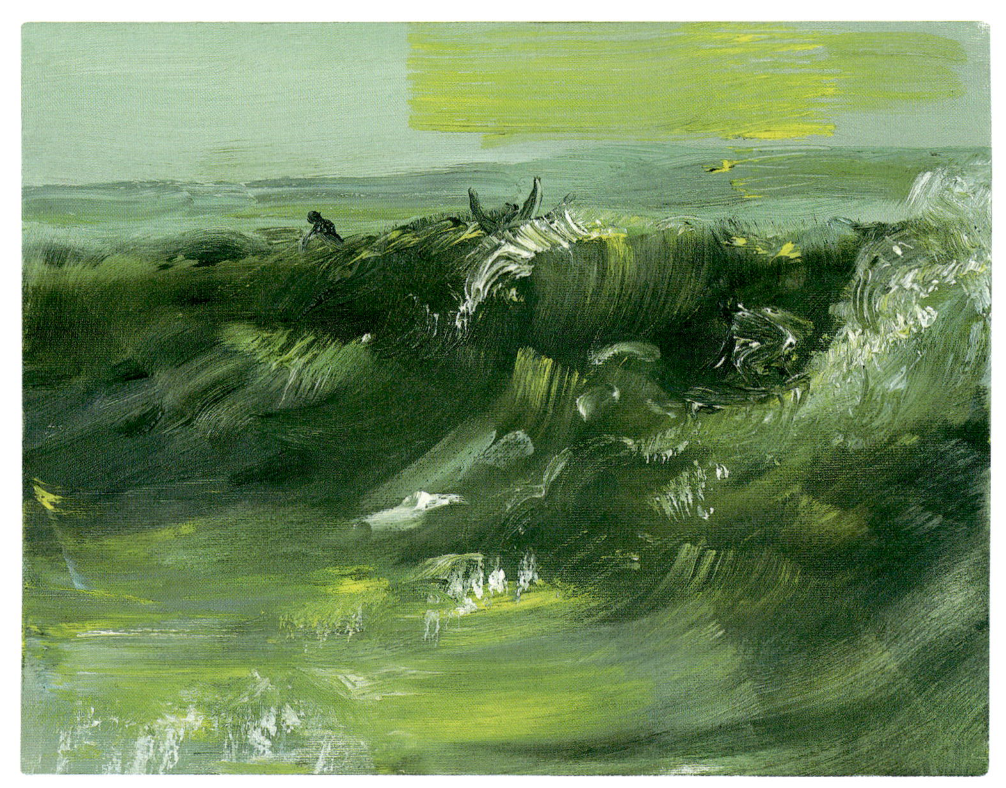

L.A. Surfscape IV, 2004

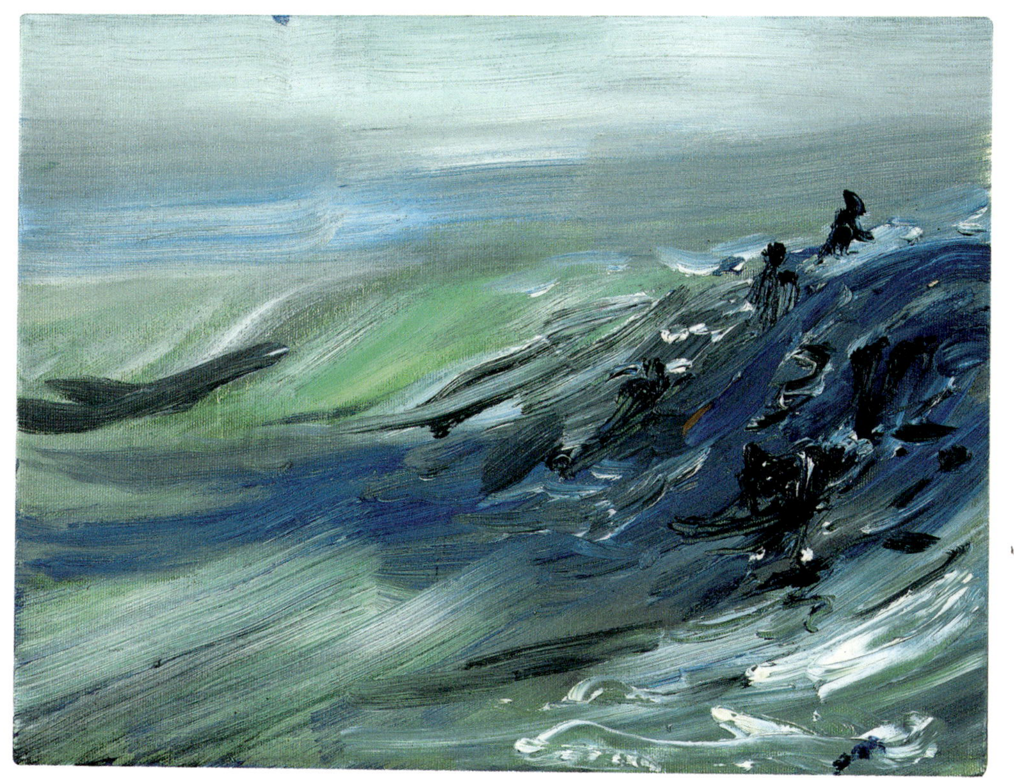

L.A. Surfscape V, 2004

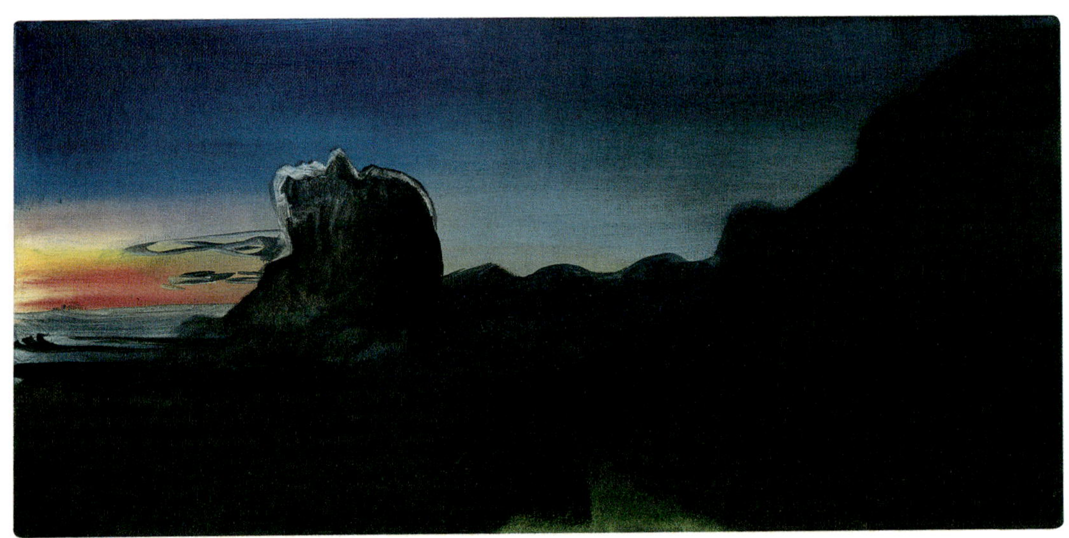

Des-Malibu Landscape, 2004   50

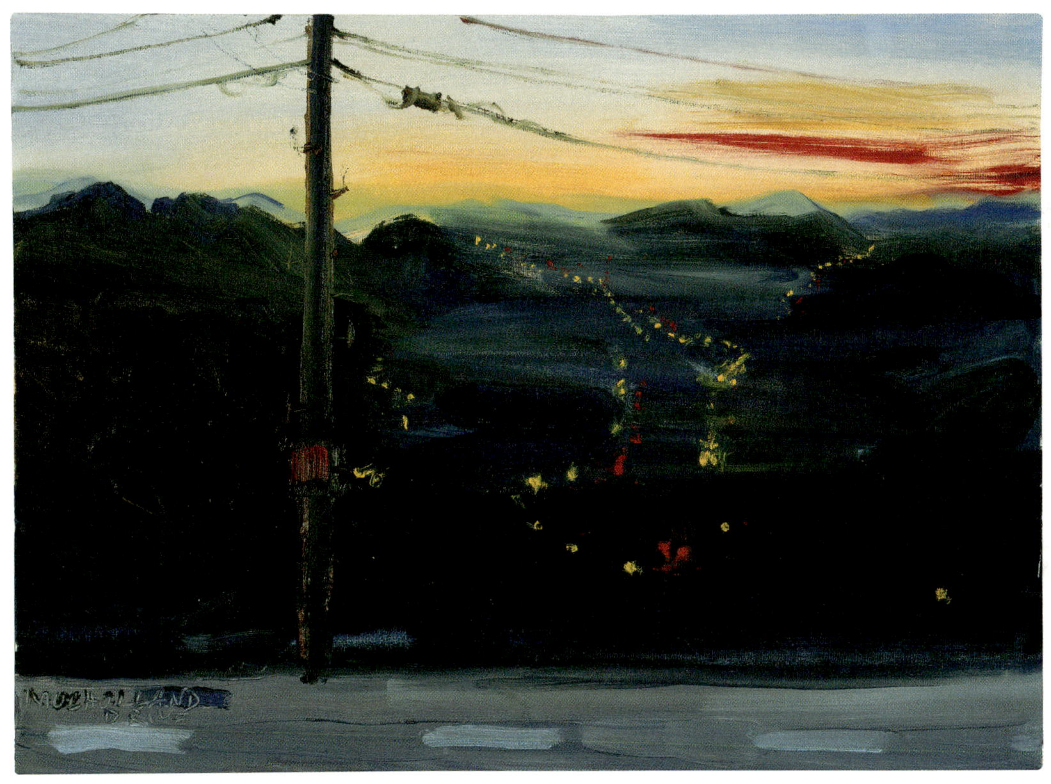

  Mulholland Drive, 2004

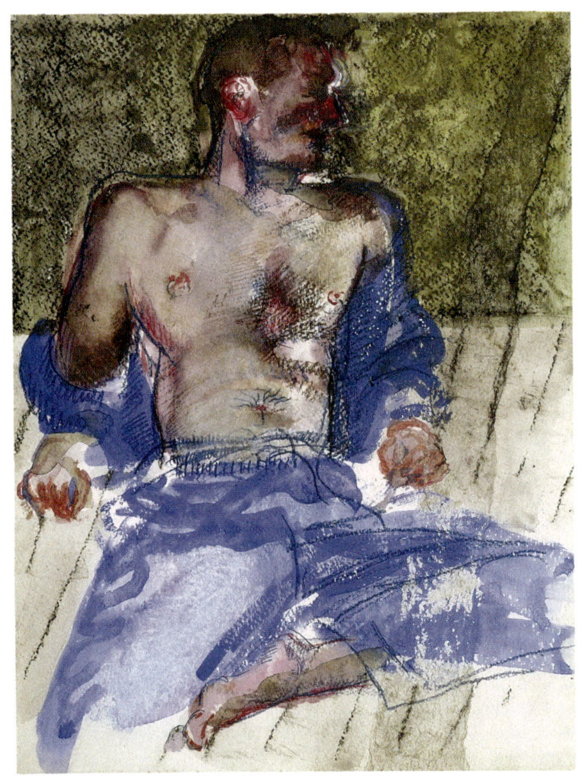

Slava, 2002

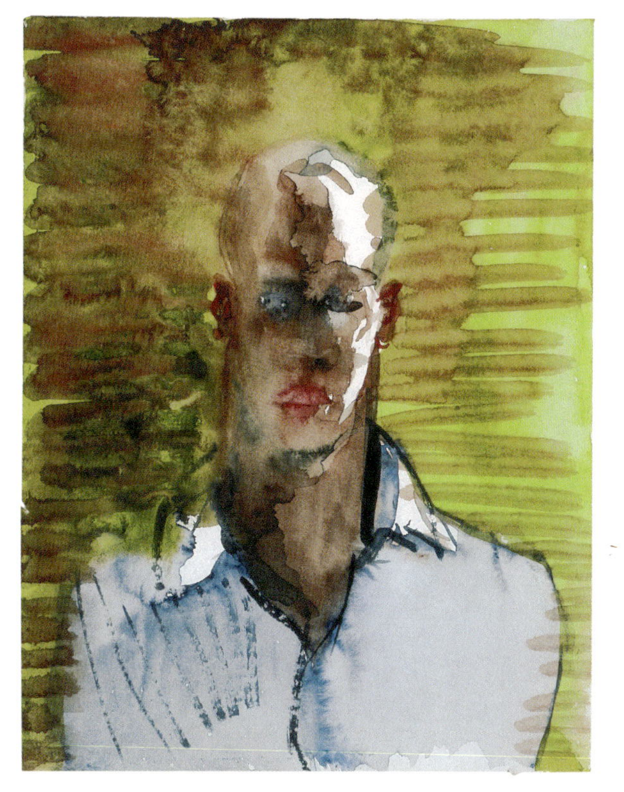

Desmond, 2003

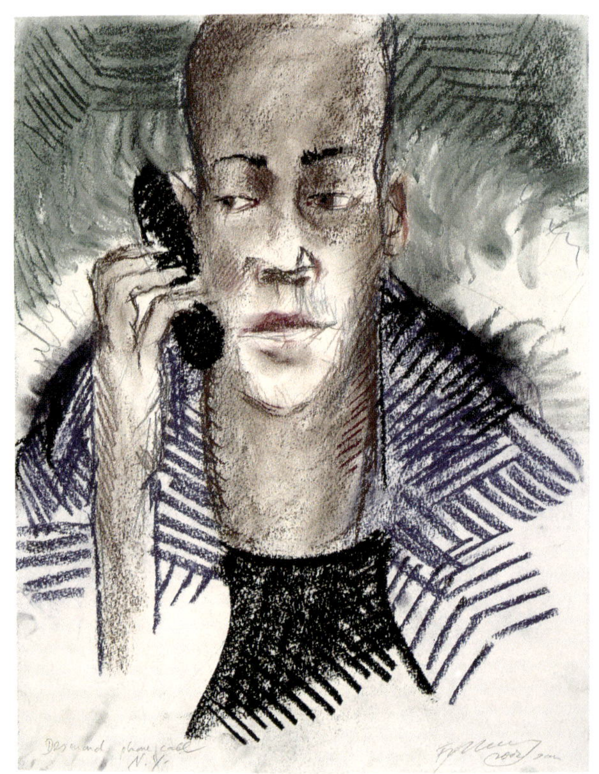

Desmond Phonecall N.Y., 2002

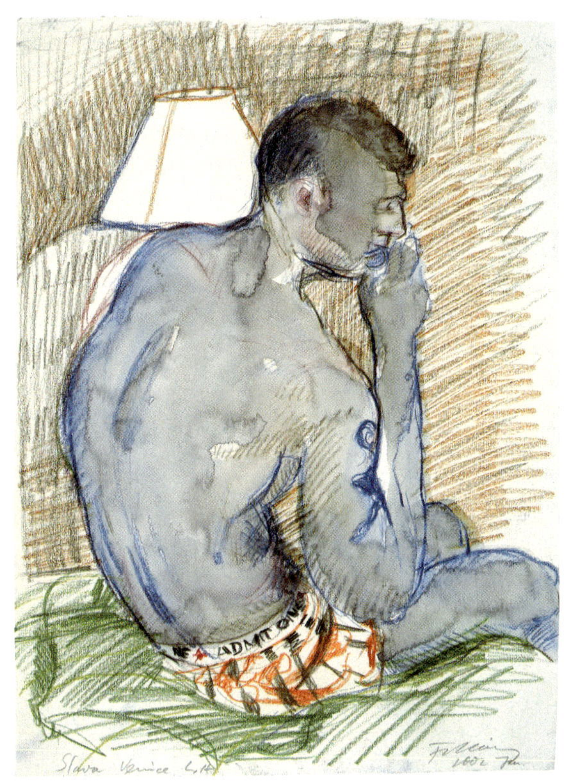

Slava Venice L.A., 2002

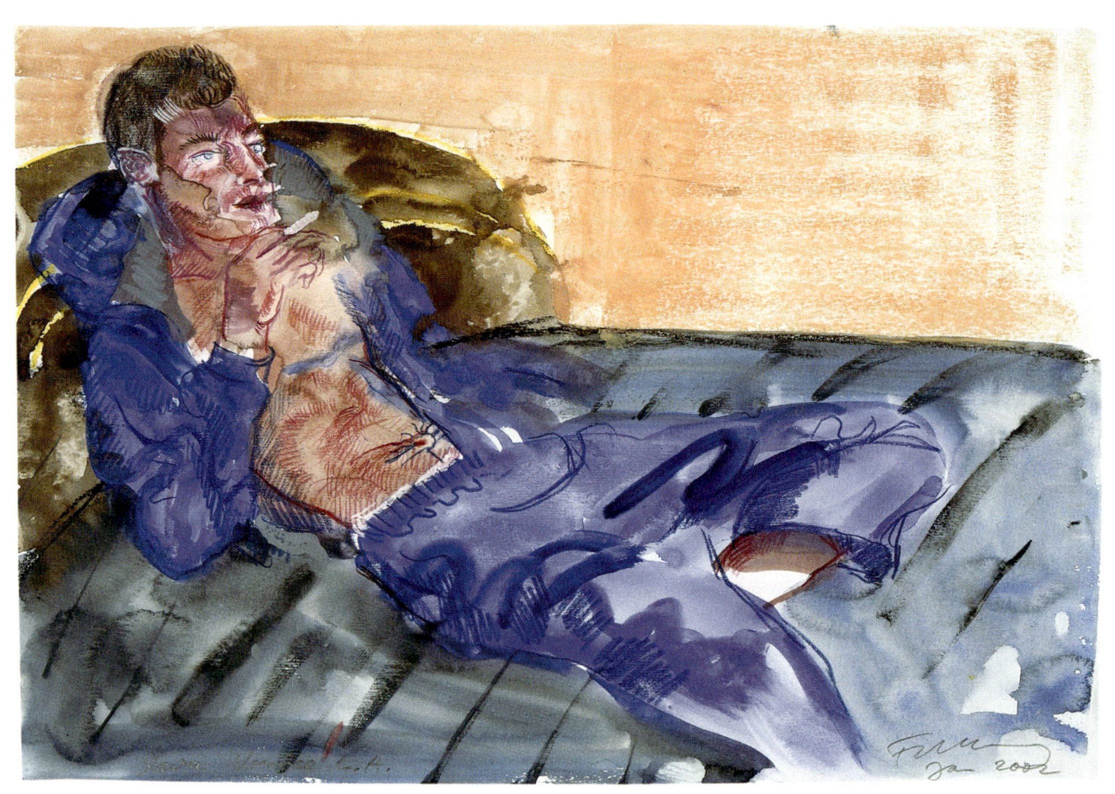

Slava Venice L.A., 2002   58

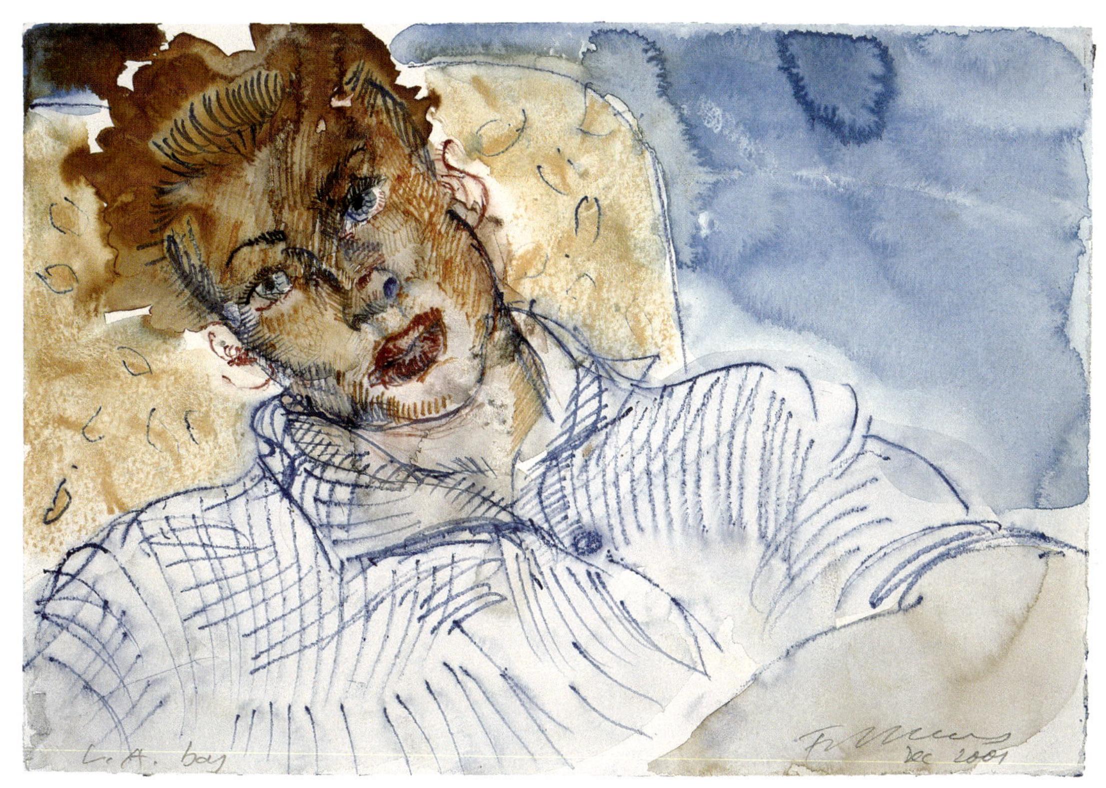

59 L.A. Boy, 2001

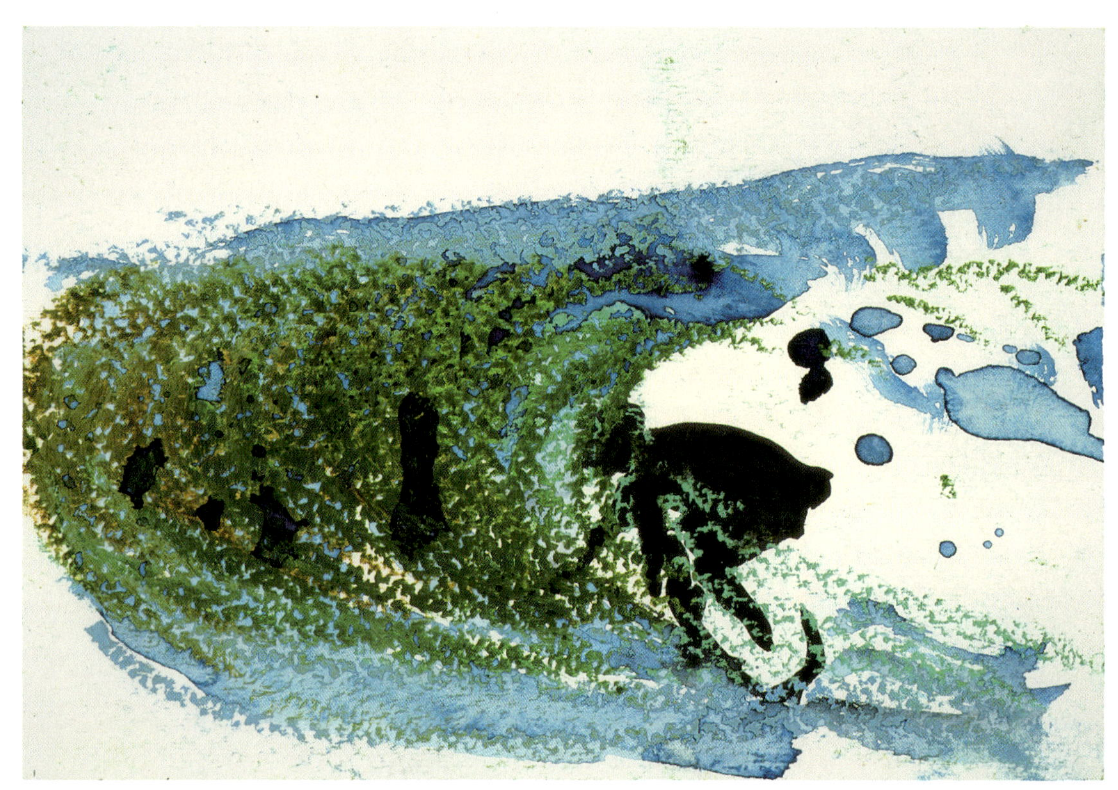

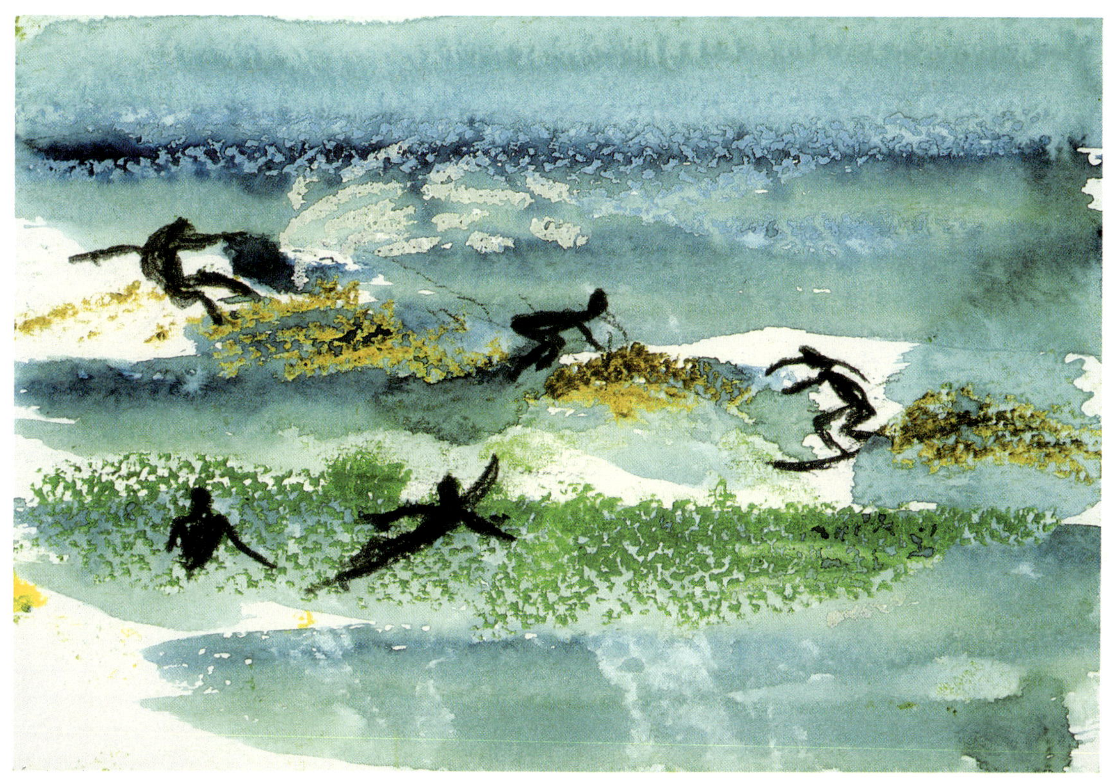

61 L.A. Surf, 2004

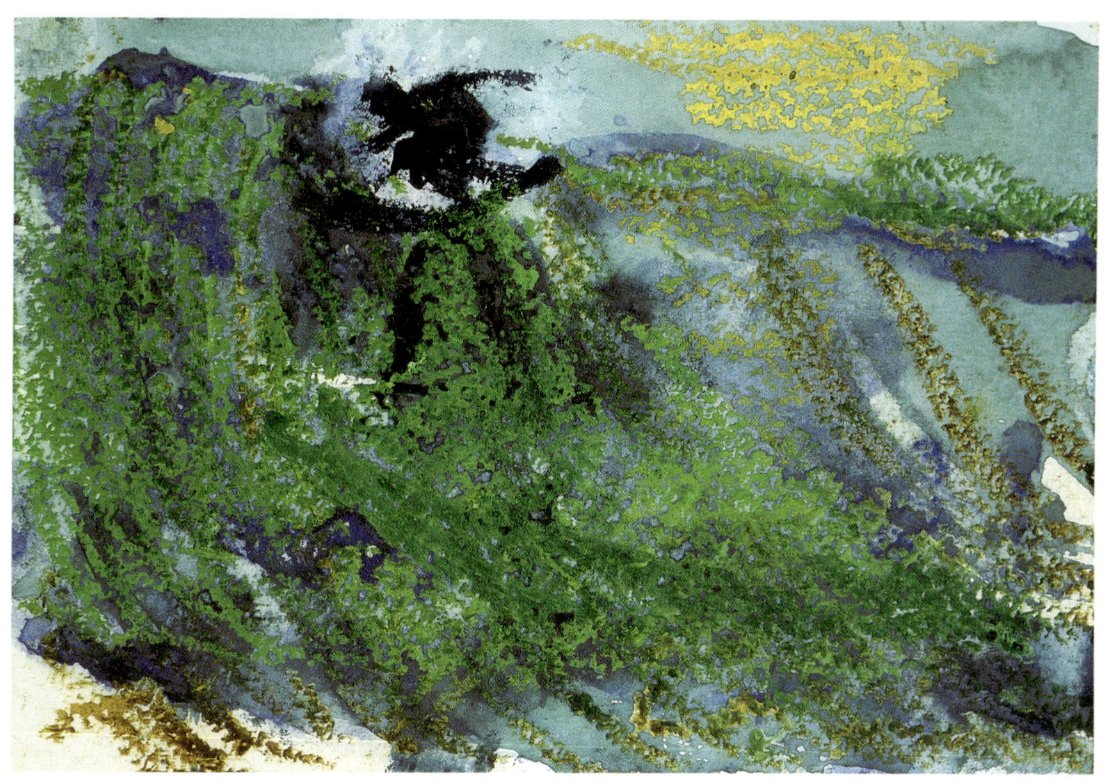

63   L.A. Surf, 2004

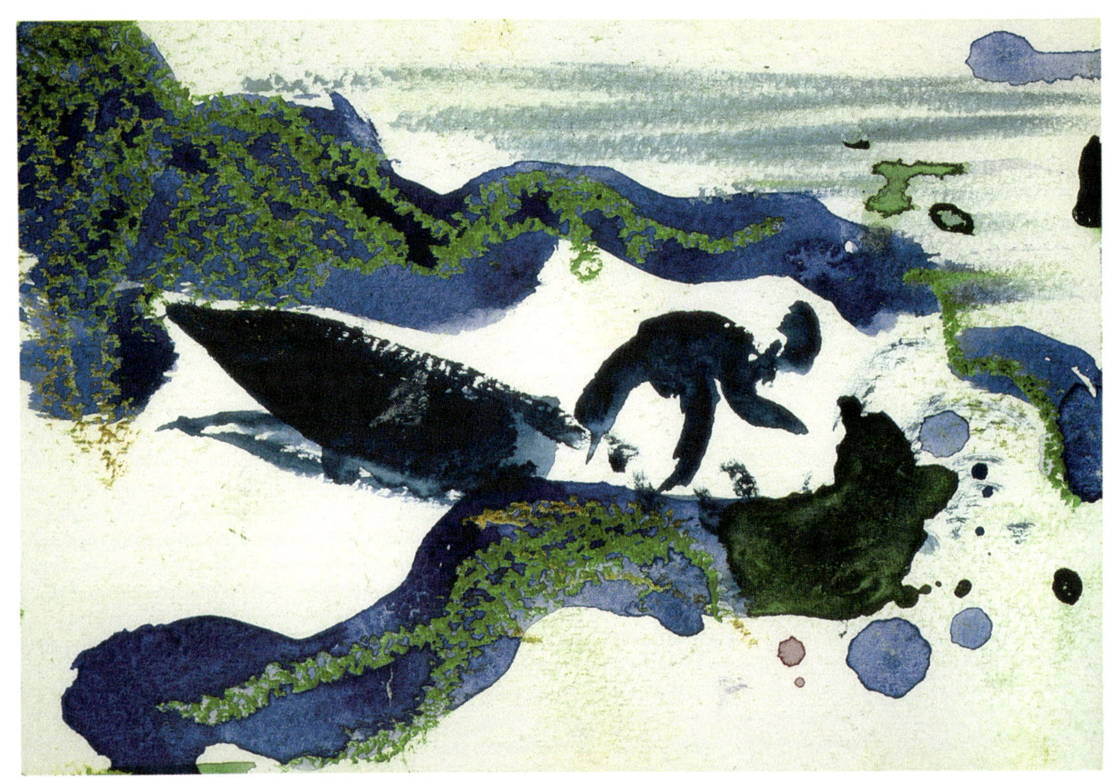

L.A. Surf, 2004

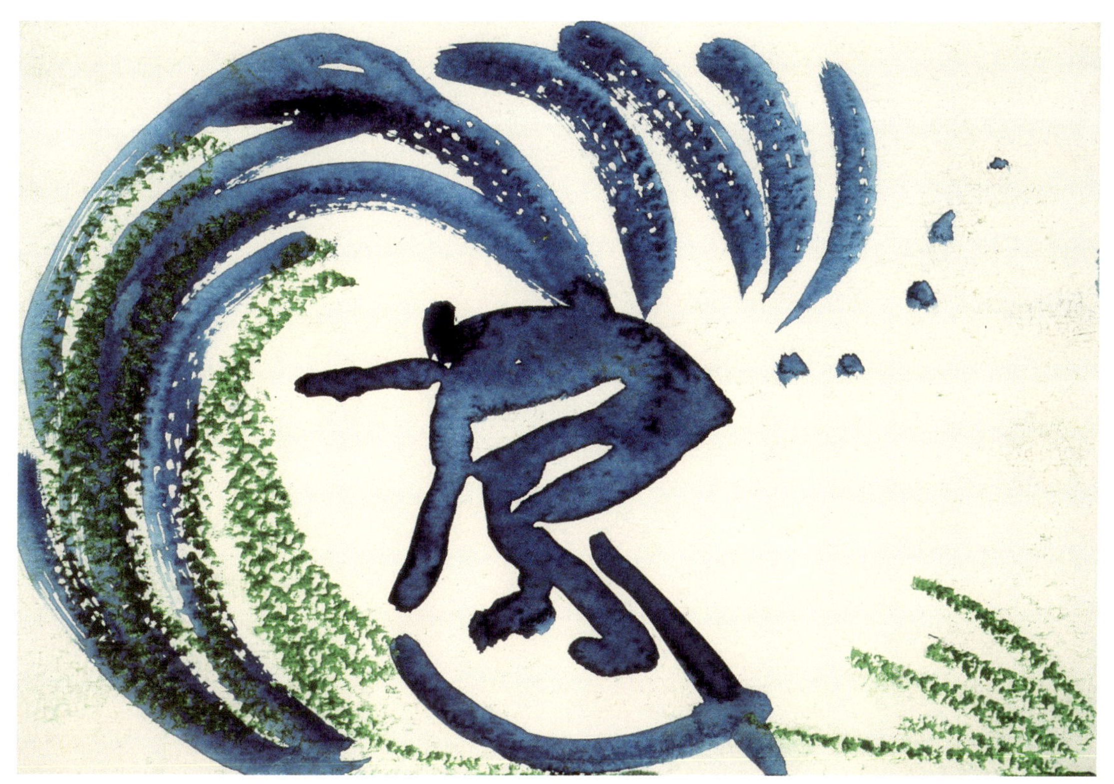

65　L.A. Surf, 2004

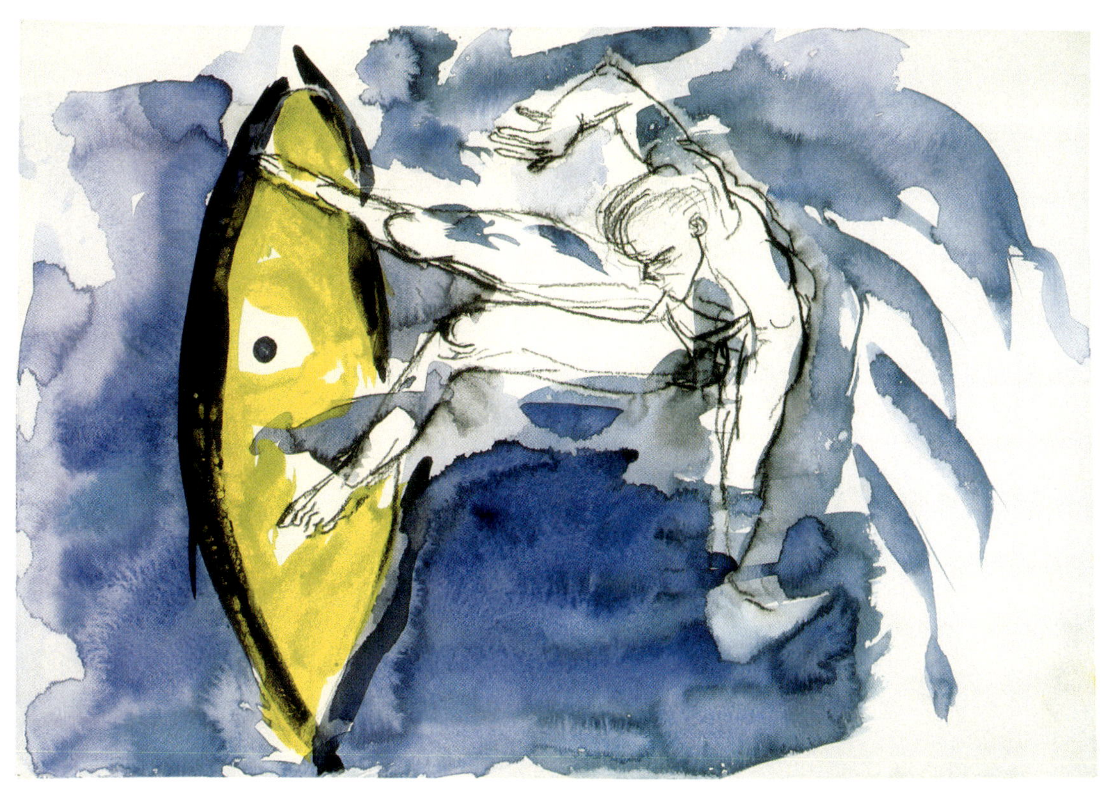

67   L.A. Surfer, 2004

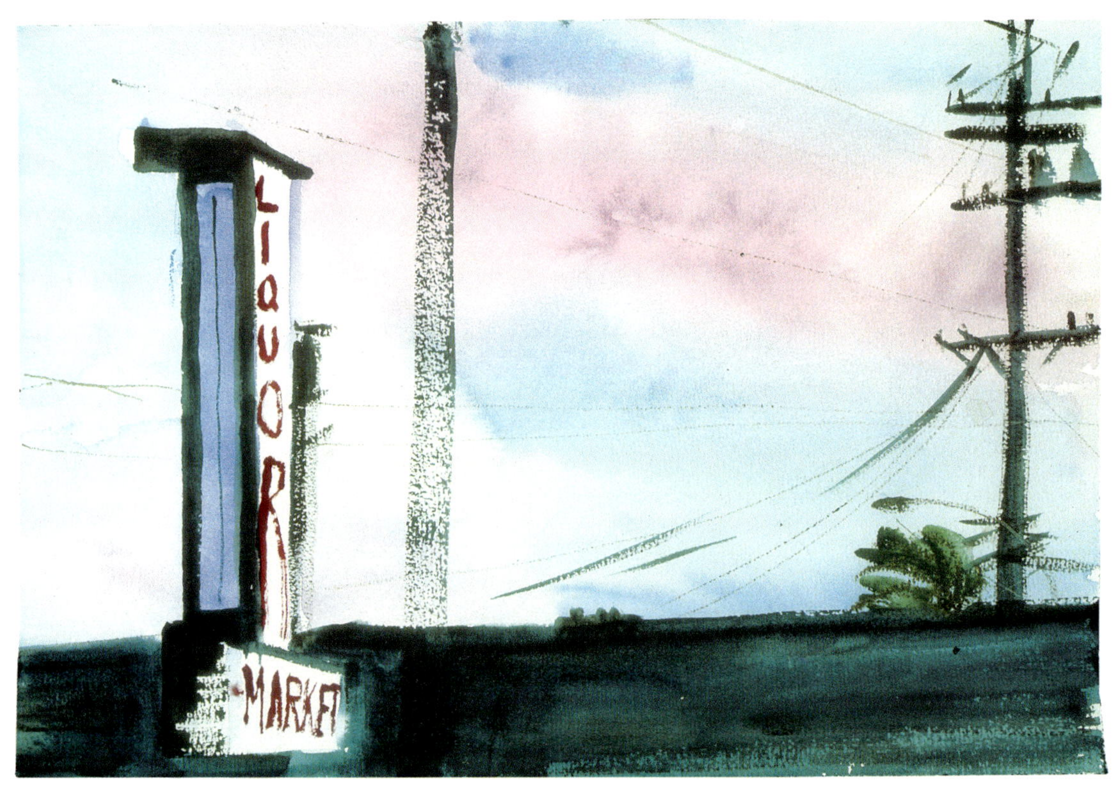

Venice Liquor, 2004

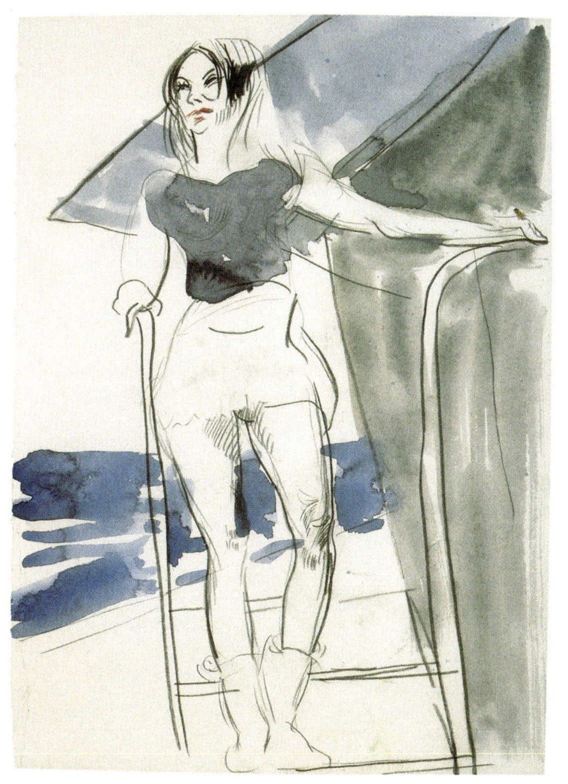

Beach Girl, 2004

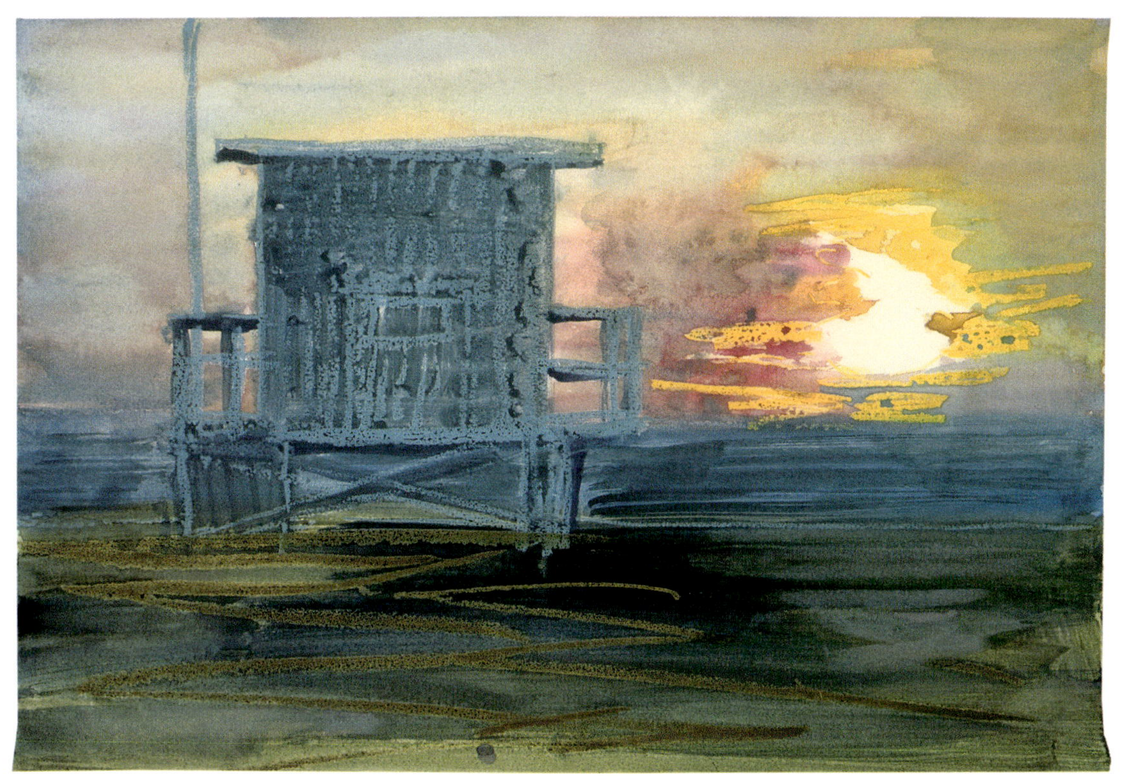

 L.A. Lifeguard Stand, 2004

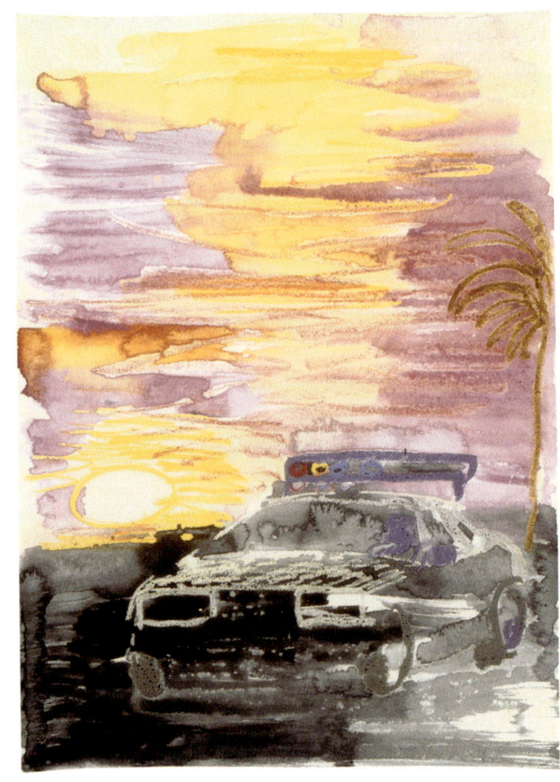

L.A. Police Car, 2004

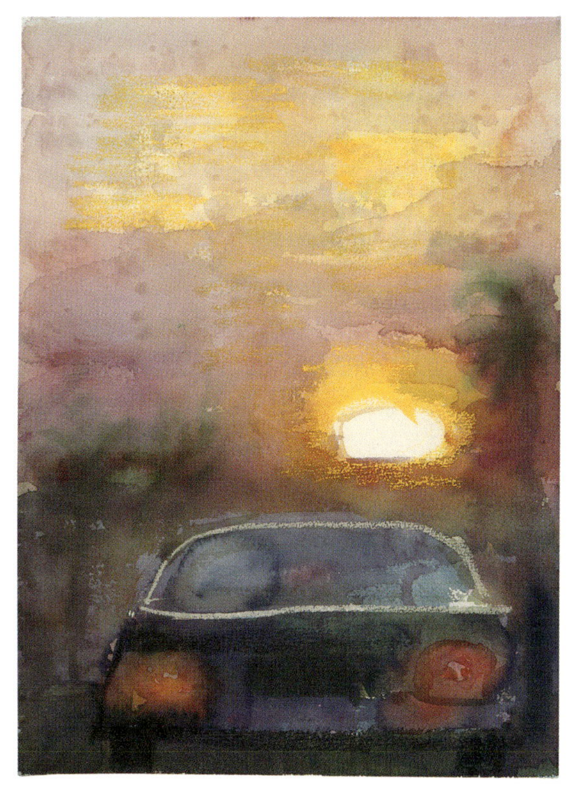

L.A. Car Sunset, 2004

Appendix

List of illustrated Works

Biography

1949   Born in **Wilhelmshaven**

1972–78   **Studied painting** under **Prof. Jaenisch** at the **Berlin Academy of Arts**

1977   **Co-founded Galerie am Moritzplatz**, Berlin
                together with **Helmut Middendorf / Salomé / Bernd Zimmer / Anne Jud / Berthold Schepers / Luciano Castelli**

1978   German Academic Exchange Service scholarship (Columbia University) to **New York**

1996   **Willy-Brandt-sculpture** for **Willy Brandt House, Berlin**

1996   **Study trip** to **Copenhagen**

Rainer Fetting lives and works in **Berlin** and **New York**

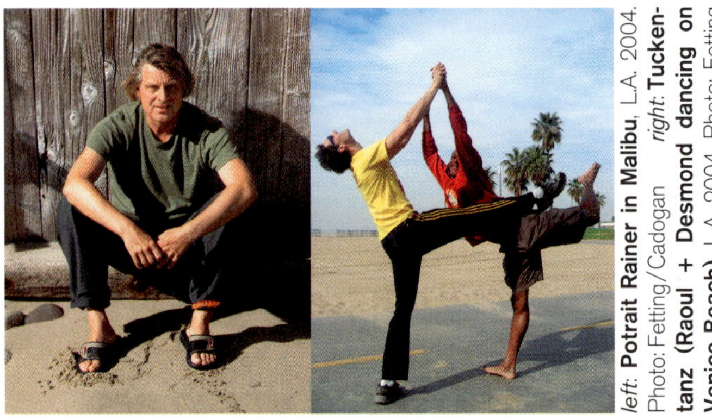

left: **Potrait Rainer in Malibu**, L.A. 2004. Photo: Fetting / Cadogan   *right:* **Tuckentanz (Raoul + Desmond dancing on Venice Beach)**, L.A. 2004. Photo: Fetting

Exhibitions

Solo exhibitions

Galerie am Moritzplatz Berlin
Anthony d'Offay London
Mary Boone New York
Bruno Bischhofberger Zurich
Paul Maenz Cologne
Yvon Lambert Paris
Studio d'Arte Cannaviello Milan
Marlborough Gallery New York
Galerie Daniel Templon Paris
Raab Galerie Berlin/London
Boukamel Contemporary Art Gallery (BCA) London
Galerie Pfefferle Munich
Galerie Tammen und Busch Berlin
Galerie Schultz Berlin
Galerie Thomas Munich

Galerie Würthle Wien
Museum Folkwang Essen
Kunsthalle Basle
Galerie Würthle Vienna
Museo di Barcelona
Staatliche Museen zu Berlin / DDR
Stadtmuseum Weimar
Galeria Gian Ferrari Arte Contemperanea Milan
Harenberg City-Center Dortmund
Martin Sanders Collection
Russian State Museum St. Petersburg
Kunsthalle Wilhelmshaven
Kunsthalle im Rathaus Munich
Kunsthalle in Emden

Group exhibitions

Haus am Waldsee Berlin
»A New Spirit in Painting«, Royal Academy of Art London
»Zeitgeist«, Martin-Gropius-Bau Berlin
Tate Gallery London
Museo de Arte Moderno Mexico City
Museum of Modern Art San Francisco
Museum of Modern Art New York

Toledo Museum of Art Toledo, Ohio
Museum of Art Tel Aviv
National Portrait Gallery London
Kunsthalle in Emden
Fondation Beyeler Riehen/Basle
ZKM Karlsruhe
Kunsthalle Vienna

Thanks to
Desmond Cadogan (New York)
Lee Hamilton (Hamilton Galleries, L.A.)
Jonathan James (L.A.)
Deborah Saron (L.A.)
Warren Long (L.A.)
Raoul Dumas (Amsterdam)
Slava Mogutin (New York)
Sebastian Zimmer (Merzig)
Bettina Giloi (L.A.)

This catalogue is published to mark the exhibition: »Rainer Fetting – Los Angeles Surfscapes«
from November 11, 2004 – January 15, 2005 at Gallery Karl Pfefferle, Munich
Gallery Karl Pfefferle Rumfordstraße 29, D – 80469 München, Tel. + 49 89 29 79 69, Fax + 49 89 291 35 71
karl.pfefferle@t-online.de, www. galeriekarlpfefferle.de

Editor: Gallery Karl Pfefferle; Concept: Kai Middendorff; Lektorat: Caroline Klapp / Bernadette Martial
Translation: Dr. Jeremy Gaines (Frankfurt / Main); Photography: Kerstin Müller / Ute Oedekoven (Berlin)
Design: Susanne Bax (Berlin); Lithography: Bayermedia (Munich)
Exhibition organisation: Iris Ortner; Exhibition design: Uwe Fischer / Kai Middendorff
Printed and published by Kerber Verlag (Bielefeld)

Kerber Verlag
Windelsbleicher Str. 166, D-33659 Bielefeld, Tel. +49 521 9500810, Fax +49 521 9500810
info@kerber-verlag.de, www.kerber-verlag.de
US Distribution: D.A.P. Distributed Art Publishers Inc., New York

ISBN 3-936646-99-6